Mr. Beat presents...

The Ultimate **American** Presidential Election **Book**

Every presidential election in U.S. history (1788-2020)

Matt Beat

Table of contents

The Presidential Election of 1788-1789

George Washington vs. **George Washington**

The very first Presidential election was the only one that took place in two different years, lasting from December 15, 1788 to Saturday, January 10, 1789. Remember, this was well before the internet, or even the telegraph, and it took days to get information around the country back then.

The extremely popular George Washington basically ran unopposed. The only real issue to be decided was who would be chosen as Vice President. Under the original Electoral College, as stated in the Constitution, each elector could vote for two people for President. The top two candidates, after adding up all the electoral votes, would be President and Vice President. Since George Washington was virtually a shoo-in, the eleven other candidates on the ballot would likely be competing for Vice President.

At this time, there were no political parties yet, and therefore no conventions. You were either a Federalist, or someone who supported the ratification of the Constitution, or an Anti-Federalist, someone who opposed its ratification. There were eleven other candidates running for President in 1788.

First, representing the Federalists were: John Adams, the famous Founding Father dude and co-writer of the Declaration of Independence from Massachusetts, John Jay, another famous Founding Father dude from New York, Robert H. Harrison, a military officer from Maryland, John Rutledge, the former Governor of South Carolina, John Hancock, the guy who wrote his name really big on the Declaration of Independence from Massachusetts, Samuel Huntington, the Governor of Connecticut, John Milton, a prominent military officer from Georgia, James

Armstrong, a state representative also from Georgia, and Benjamin Lincoln, the former Continental States Secretary of War from Massachusetts.

Next, representing the Anti-Federalists were: George Clinton, the popular Governor of New York, and Edward Telfair, the Governor of Georgia.

John Adams was the clear favorite to get second place to Washington. Alexander Hamilton, who couldn't run himself since he was born outside the former colonies, feared that if John Adams was also the unanimous choice, he would end in a tie with Washington and might even become president, which would be embarrassing for the new electoral system. Therefore, Hamilton talked electors into voting for other candidates.

And here are the results...

George Washington won, becoming the very first United States President.

Washington was the only President in history to win 100 percent of the electoral votes. That means every single elector voted for him. Washington received 69 electoral votes; John Adams received 34, enough to become the first Vice President; John Jay received 9; and everyone else received 6 or less. The Federalists clearly dominated this election, with only three Anti-Federalist electors winning in the entire country.

It's important to note that four states did not participate in this first Presidential election. North Carolina and Rhode Island had not yet ratified the Constitution, the New York legislature was deadlocked, and Vermont was operating as an unrecognized state at the time of this election.

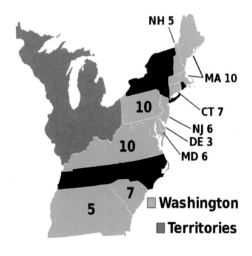

Turn the page for the next election, buddy.

The Presidential Election of 1792

vs.

George Washington **George Washington**

The second Presidential election in American history was held from Friday, November 2 to Wednesday, December 5, 1792. It marked the first time an incumbent was trying to get reelected. Well, George Washington was that incumbent, and he wouldn't have much stopping him. Just like in his first Presidential election, Washington essentially ran unopposed.

Here are some fun facts! This election was the first in which each of the original 13 states appointed electors. The new states of Kentucky and Vermont also had electors. It was also the only presidential election that was not held exactly four years after the previous election.

By 1792, the first two major political parties had formed– the Federalist Party, led by Treasury Secretary Alexander Hamilton, and the Democratic Republican Party, led by Secretary of State Thomas Jefferson and U.S. Representative James Madison. As you might have guessed, most of the former Federalists joined Hamilton's Federalist Party, calling for a more unified country and stronger federal government. Most of the former Anti-Federalists, or the ones who thought the Constitution gave the federal government too much power, ended up joining the Democratic Republican Party.

Although George Washington had considered retiring, both sides encouraged him to run for reelection to unite a quickly dividing country. Again, under the original Electoral College, each elector could vote for two people for President. The top two candidates, after adding up all the electoral votes, would be President and Vice President. So, while Washington faced no serious threat, there *was* a close race for second between the current Vice President and Federalist John Adams and the Governor of New York and Democratic Republican George Clinton.

The Democratic Republicans would have preferred to nominate Thomas Jefferson, but this would have cost them the state of Virginia, as electors were not permitted to vote for two candidates from their home state, and Washington was also from Virginia. Despite this, some who did not like Clinton voted for Jefferson and fellow Democratic Republican Aaron Burr, anyway.

And here are the results...

George Washington won, remaining the first American President. Are you really that surprised? Again, he received 100 percent of the electoral votes. Wow! Imagine that happening today.

John Adams again finished in second place, receiving 77 of the electoral votes and remaining our first Vice President. Future Vice President George Clinton finished third, receiving 50 electoral votes (spoiler alert), future President Thomas Jefferson finished fourth, receiving four electoral votes (double spoiler alert), and future Vice President Aaron Burr finished fifth, receiving one electoral vote (triple spoiler alert).

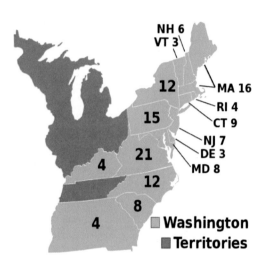

Although the popular vote meant very little in 1792 due to many voting restrictions, Federalists won 91% of the vote, easily dominating over the Democratic Republicans.

About 0.88% of the population voted in this election, a record low turnout for a United States presidential election.

Turn the page for the next election, buddy.

The Presidential Election of 1796

John Adams   vs.   Thomas Jefferson

The third Presidential election in American history was held from Friday, November 4 to Wednesday, December 7, 1796. Incumbent President George Washington refused to run for a third term, setting a precedent that would last until 1940. Without Washington, who most Americans loved, this created a big void, and twelve different candidates all competed for President and Vice President. Needless to say, Americans were a bit nervous about this one.

Again, under the original Electoral College, each elector could vote for two people for President. The top two candidates, after adding up all the electoral votes, would be President and Vice President.

There were seven Federalist Party candidates and five Democratic Republican Party candidates. They each technically ran alone, as the formal position of a running mate didn't exist yet. While incumbent Vice President John Adams was the leading candidate for the Federalists, and former Secretary of State Thomas Jefferson was the leading candidate for the Democratic Republicans, both parties ran multiple candidates for President, hoping to keep one of their opponents from being the runner-up.

The other Federalist candidates were: Thomas Pinckney, the former governor of South Carolina, Oliver Ellsworth, a former U.S. Senator and current U.S. Supreme Court Chief Justice from Connecticut, John Jay, the current Governor of New York, James Iredell, a U.S. Supreme Court Justice from North Carolina, Samuel Johnston, a former U.S. Senator also from North Carolina, and Charles Cotesworth Pinckney, the U.S. Minister to France from South Carolina. Yeah, Thomas Pinckney and Charles Cotesworth Pinckney were brothers.

The other Democratic Republican candidates were: Aaron Burr, a U.S. Senator from New York, Samuel Adams, the current Governor of Massachusetts, but more famously the American Revolution leader and second cousin to John Adams, John Henry, a U.S. Senator from Maryland, and George Clinton, the now former governor of New York. Clinton refused to run, but people campaigned for him anyway.

Unlike the 1792 election, when everyone knew George Washington was going to win, the election of 1796 was up in the air. Because of this, this was the first election where there was heavy campaigning on both sides, with the Democratic Republicans mostly campaigning for Jefferson, and Federalists mostly campaigning for Adams. The campaigns began to get nasty and angry, with Federalists associating Democratic Republicans with the violence of the French Revolution and Democratic Republicans accusing Federalists of being too cozy with Britain.

Since the 1792 election, Tennessee had joined the United States, increasing the Electoral College to 138 electors.

And here are the results...

John Adams won, receiving 71 electoral votes. He became the second President of the United States.

Thomas Jefferson finished second, receiving 68 electoral votes. He became the second Vice President. Wait a second, what? Two main opponents together? Awkward. Yep, this election was the only one in which a president and vice president were elected from opposing tickets, and would be a big reason why the Twelfth Amendment to the Constitution was later ratified.

Alexander Hamilton might have unintentionally helped cause this awkward situation. Trying to go against Adams, Hamilton attempted to convince people to throw a vote to Jefferson in order to get Pinckney elected instead of Adams. This, combined with the fact that many Adams electors failed to cast their second vote for Pinckney, caused the unique result.

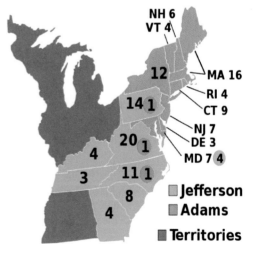

Interestingly, several other candidates also received a high number of electoral votes. Thomas Pinckney received 59 electoral votes, Aaron Burr received 30, Sam Adams received 15, Oliver Ellsworth received 11, George Clinton received seven, and everyone else received five or less. Despite the fact that George Washington did not run, he still received two electoral votes.

Compared to the 1792 election, Democratic Republicans made significant gains in 1796, though it's difficult to pinpoint how much since just seven states allowed popular voting in the election.

About 2.07% of the population voted in this election.

Turn the page for the next election, buddy.

The Presidential Election of 1800

vs.

John Adams

Thomas Jefferson

The fourth Presidential election in American history was held from Friday, October 31 to Wednesday, December 3, 1800.

It was a significant election. In fact, some called it the "Revolution of 1800" due to the political realignment it created. It was essentially a rematch between incumbent President John Adams and his off-and-on friend/enemy Vice President Thomas Jefferson.

In 1800, Adams and Jefferson were far from friends. The two had spent the previous four years awkwardly working side-by-side as President and Vice President, but now they seemed to hate each other. Their campaigns were just plain nasty. Jefferson supporters said President Adams had a "hideous hermaphroditical character which has neither the force and firmness of a man nor the gentleness and sensibility of a woman." Adams supporters responded by calling Vice President Jefferson "a mean-spirited son of a half-breed Indian squaw, sired by a Virginia mulatto father." Federalists called Jefferson a "bad Christian," who had too much sympathy for the French Revolution, while Democratic Republicans said that Adams was giving too much power to the federal government, talking trash about his signing of the Alien and Sedition Acts and his expansion of the military.

With this election, political parties officially chose running mates for Adams and Jefferson, hoping they each would be elected the Vice President, therefore avoiding another embarrassing result like the one after the election of 1796, where two dudes with opposite views were in the executive branch together. The Federalists chose Charles Cotesworth Pinckney as Adams' running mate, and the Democratic Republicans chose Aaron Burr.

Remember, under the original Electoral College, each elector could vote for two people for President. The top two candidates would be President and Vice President.

And here are the results...

First of all, it's important to note that the results were heavily disputed. However, Thomas Jefferson and Aaron Burr both received 73 electoral votes, ensuring the Democratic Republican victory. One of the Democratic Republican electors was supposed to not vote for Burr, but he did anyway. So with Jefferson and Burr tied, the House of Representatives had to choose one of them to become President. With the influence of Alexander Hamilton, the still mostly Federalist House went with Jefferson. While Hamilton didn't like Jefferson, he straight up hated and was afraid of Burr. Hamilton once called Burr "one of the worst men in the community."

Jefferson became the third President and Aaron Burr became the third Vice President in American history. John Adams became the first one-term President when he received 65 electoral votes. The Federalists planned a bit better by giving 64 electoral votes to Charles Cotesworth Pinckney and one electoral vote to John Jay (who officially now lost his fourth consecutive Presidential election).

NH 6
VT 4
12
MA 16
RI 4
CT 9
8 7
NJ 7
DE 3
4
21
MD 5 5
3
8 4
8
☐ Jefferson
4
☐ Adams
■ Territories

This election was significant because it was the first peaceful transition of political power between opposing parties in American history. It was also a turning point. It marked the beginning of a generation of Democratic Republican party rule, and the beginning of the decline of the Federalist Party, who would never again have a President in office. The result of this election was affected by the Three-Fifths Compromise. Had slaves not been counted for purposes of congressional apportionment, Adams would have beat Jefferson. However, Jefferson still would have won the popular vote.

About 1.52% of the population voted in this election.

Turn the page for the next election, buddy.

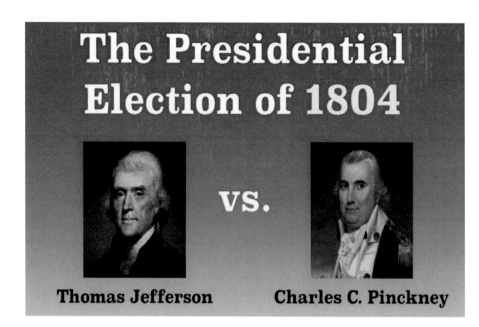

The Presidential Election of 1804

vs.

Thomas Jefferson   **Charles C. Pinckney**

The fifth Presidential election in American history was held from Friday, November 2, to Wednesday, December 5, 1804. Incumbent President Thomas Jefferson sought reelection. Jefferson, the Democratic Republican candidate, had become very popular during his four years as President. He kept most of his promises, rolling back the expansion of the federal government, getting rid of the whiskey tax, and repealing the remaining provisions of the Alien and Sedition Acts, even pardoning all ten individuals who had been prosecuted under the laws. He made Federalists angry but most Americans happy with the Louisiana Purchase, which doubled the size of the country. He handled foreign conflicts with relative ease, standing up to the Barbary pirates.

So for this election, his main opponent, the Federalist Party candidate Charles Cotesworth Pinckney, had quite the challenge trying to convince voters to swing his way. A hero of the Revolutionary War and a former Ambassador to France, Pinckney had previously ran for President, but now was finally the Federalist frontrunner.

The election was significant because it was the first one after the ratification of the Twelfth Amendment to the Constitution. The Twelfth Amendment says presidential electors have to give their choice for both President and Vice President on their ballots. No longer would the second place winner be the Vice President.

The Democratic Republicans chose a new running mate for Jefferson- George Clinton. Wait a second, what happened to Burr, Jefferson's Vice President? Well, Jefferson and Burr had a shaky relationship throughout the first term. Oh yeah, and Burr had shot and killed Alexander

Hamilton in a duel earlier in the year. Jefferson had understandably distanced himself from Burr after that.

The Federalists nominated Massachusetts legend and Founding Father dude Rufus King as Pinckney's running mate. The Federalist Party seemed sort of afraid to run against Jefferson in 1804 and ran a weak campaign. Most predicted Jefferson would win the election by a big margin.

In 1804, there was another important change- Ohio was now part of the Presidential election process after becoming a state the previous year.

And here are the results...

Thomas Jefferson didn't just win the election by a big margin. He won it by a *huge* margin, remaining the third President in American history. Jefferson received 162 electoral votes, compared to Pinckney receiving just 14 electoral votes.

Jefferson won all states except for Delaware and Connecticut. New England states had previously almost always voted for whoever the Federalist candidate was. Not so much this time, and this was another big blow to the Federalist Party. George Clinton was elected as the country's fourth Vice President.

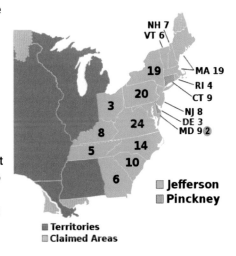

With this election, Jefferson became the first former Vice President in American history to be elected and then reelected, and only one of two Americans to ever accomplish such a feat. Jefferson's 45.6 percentage point victory margin in the popular vote remains the most lopsided in American history. In other words, since then the victory margin has not been so high in a presidential election with multiple major party candidates.

About 3.24% of the population voted in this election.

Turn the page for the next election, buddy.

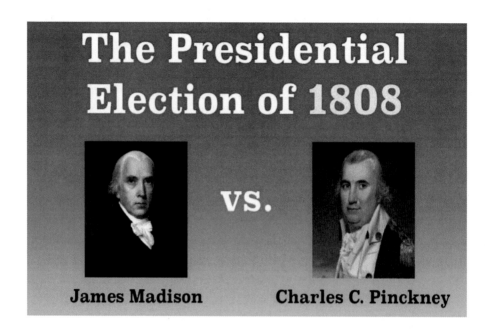

The Presidential Election of 1808

James Madison   vs.   Charles C. Pinckney

The sixth Presidential election in American history was held from Friday, November 4, to Wednesday, December 7, 1808. Like George Washington before him, Thomas Jefferson decided not to seek a third term. Jefferson's second term did not go as smoothly as his first, and a growing number of Americans, especially New England merchants, were happy to see him gone thanks to the unpopular Embargo Act of 1807. Still, Jefferson had remained fairly popular, and Democratic Republicans hoped to continue to ride the tide of his popularity to stay in power.

Congressional caucuses decided nominations for President and Vice President in 1808. Secretary of State James Madison, diplomat James Monroe, and Vice President George Clinton were all in the running to be the Democratic Republican Presidential nominee, but it was Madison who won the nomination. Although John Quincy Adams, a U.S. Senator from Massachusetts and son of former President John Adams, Henry Dearborn, the U.S. Secretary of War, and John Langdon, the Governor of New Hampshire and Founding Father dude, were in the running, George Clinton was voted to remain the Vice President. Even though Clinton didn't want to run for President (again), some people started a campaign for him anyway (again).

The Federalist caucus had apparently forgotten the butt-kicking they received in the Presidential election of 1804, so they once again nominated the same candidates in 1808- former Minister to France Charles Cotesworth Pinckney for President, and former U.S. Senator and Founding Father dude Rufus King for Vice President. Maybe the Federalists were confident that the anger directed toward Jefferson because of the Embargo Act would carry over to James Madison?

And here are the results...

James Madison won, becoming the fourth President in American history. It was another solid victory for the Democratic Republicans. Madison received 122 electoral votes. Pinckney and King made solid gains from 1804, but Pinckney still only received 47 electoral votes, well less than half the votes that Madison got. Interestingly, some Democratic Republican electors refused to cast their votes for Madison. George Clinton received six of those electoral votes, which was kind of weird, since he also was reelected as Vice President. In fact, this election was the first of only two times in American history where a new President would be elected but the incumbent Vice President would continue to stay in office. To protest Clinton's run for President, nine electors chose John Langdon to be Madison's Vice President instead of him. So essentially, four people were in the running for President and/or Vice President in 1808.

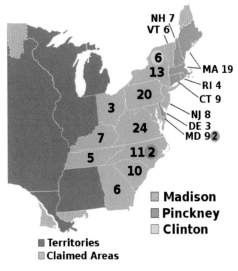

Additionally, James Monroe earned three electoral votes for Vice President and 2.5% of the popular vote for President. Speaking of the popular vote, Madison received 64.7% and Pinckney received 32.4%, and all others received less than 1% of the popular vote. Either way, Democratic Republicans still dominated.

The presidential election of 1808 was the last one in which Virginia had the most electoral votes. New York would have the most for the next 160 years.

4.36% of the population voted in this election.

Turn the page for the next election, buddy.

The Presidential Election of 1812

VS.

James Madison   **DeWitt Clinton**

The seventh Presidential election in American history took place from Friday, October 30 to Wednesday, December 2, 1812. It was the first Presidential election after Louisiana became a state, and it was also the first one that took place when the country was at war. It was the War of 1812, as matter of fact, which was one of the most creative names of a war ever.

In June, incumbent James Madison had given into the pressure of the War Hawks and asked Congress to declare war on the United Kingdom. However, the United States struggled at the beginning of the war against the clearly superior British forces.

A growing number of Democratic Republicans were not happy with Madison and refused to support his renomination. Instead, they supported Dewitt Clinton for President. Dewitt was the nephew of Madison's former Vice President, George Clinton, who had died earlier that year. He was also a former U.S. Senator representing New York and the mayor of New York City. The New York Democratic Republican caucus almost unanimously nominated Clinton for President. So there was a split in the Democratic Republican party between the Madison supporters and the Clinton supporters.

The Federalists for a time considered nominating Chief Justice John Marshall for President, but after Clinton entered the race as an alternative to Madison, many decided to endorse him instead. Whenever two or more political parties on a ballot list the same candidate, by the way, that's called electoral fusion. Still, some Federalists refused to support the nomination of Clinton, and instead nominated former U.S. Senator and Founding Father dude Rufus King.

Dewitt Clinton was an interesting candidate because he seemingly said whatever was needed to make both Federalists and Democratic Republicans happy. That's right, he told whatever crowd he was in front of whatever they wanted to hear. For example, when he was in New England, he would pander to the Federalists by saying he was against the war, but when he was out west where many Democratic Republicans were, he talked as if he seemingly was just fine with the war.

Clinton's running mate was the Attorney General of Pennsylvania and Founding Father dude Jared Ingersoll. Madison's running mate was Elbridge Gerry, another Founding Father dude and Massachusetts Governor who is a big reason why we have the Bill of Rights. I should also mention that he was the one who signed a bill redistricting Massachusetts to help his Democratic Republican candidates get elected, which was the first notable example of gerrymandering, named after him of course.

Anyway, because of the fusion support for Clinton, many believed Madison would not get to keep his job.

And here are the results...

James Madison won reelection, with 50.4% of the popular vote. Dewitt Clinton won 47.6% of the popular vote. It was the closest Presidential election up to that point for the popular vote. Rufus King received 2% of the popular vote. Looking at the electoral vote, it's not nearly as close, with Madison receiving 128 electoral votes to Clinton's 89 electoral votes.

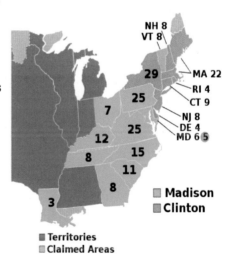

Madison remained the fourth President in American history, and Elbridge Gerry became the fifth Vice President in American history. Madison was one of the few Presidents in American history to win reelection with less support than his first election. But a win is a win, right?

4.61% of the population voted in this election.

Turn the page for the next election buddy.

The Presidential Election of 1816

vs.

James Monroe   **Rufus King**

The eighth Presidential election in American history took place from Friday, November 1 to Wednesday, December 4, 1816. Deciding to play it cool like his predecessors Thomas Jefferson and George Washington, President James Madison decided not to run for a third term.

Madison's second term had been heavily influenced by the War of 1812, and he proved to be a solid leader during it. After the war was over, even though the United States hadn't technically won, Americans still felt pretty good about how they were able to defend themselves against the British, all things considered. It was the beginning of the so-called Era of Good Feelings, and the patriotism that swept the country during that time at least temporarily helped unite it. Simply put, Madison was popular and James Monroe, Madison's Secretary of State who now wanted to take Madison's place, was also popular.

The Federalists, meanwhile, were not so popular. Because many of them talked trash about involvement in the war, and especially because some of them even talked about seceding from the Union at the series of meetings known as the Hartford Convention, many Americans turned their backs on the Federalist Party. Ironically, the biggest complaints at the Hartford Convention stemmed from the fact that the federal government was gaining too much power. In fact, Madison had changed his mind on things so much when he was President that made him seem more like a traditional Federalist. For example, he began favoring a national bank and protective tariffs. If prominent Democratic Republicans were now acting like Federalists, what was the point of having both parties?

The Federalists didn't even officially nominate anyone for President in 1816. With the Federalist Party now out of the picture, the Democratic Republicans prepared for a landslide victory. Several names popped up other than James Monroe for the nomination. Many wanted rising star Henry Clay, the Speaker of the House, and the Battle of New Orleans hero Andrew Jackson to run, but both declined. William H. Crawford, the U.S. Secretary of War, really thought about running, but knew he stood no chance against Monroe so decided not to. Pennsylvania Governor Simon Snyder and New York Governor Daniel D. Tompkins both ran but withdrew before the Democratic Republican caucus. Even though Monroe was widely loved, there was a growing number who didn't want him to get the nomination because he was yet another dude from Virginia. Indeed, some were weary of the so-called "Virginia dynasty."

Still, James Monroe got the nomination, which almost guaranteed him the Presidency. Or did it? Monroe's running mate was Daniel D. Tompkins. I mentioned him earlier. Weren't you paying attention? Gosh!

Like I mentioned before, the Federalists didn't formally nominate anyone, but many Federalists again supported Rufus King, the former U.S. Senator and Founding Father dude, with John Eager Howard, a former U.S. Senator from Maryland, as his running mate this time.

And here are the results...

First, there was a bit of conflict. When people voted in November and December, Indiana wasn't officially a state yet, but its citizens wanted their votes to be counted, too. Some argued their votes shouldn't be counted as Indiana was still technically a territory during the election period. Long story short, Indiana got its way, and its votes were counted.

It is no surprise here, but James Monroe won the election, becoming the fifth President of the United States. Monroe received 183 electoral votes, with Rufus King receiving just 34 electoral votes. Monroe was the second James in a row to win the Presidency. In fact, James would prove to be the most popular first name of Presidents throughout American history, with four more dudes named "James" being elected President as well.

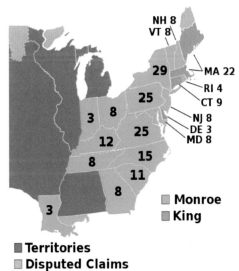

Daniel D. Tompkins became the sixth Vice President in American history.

Monroe won 68.2 percent of the popular vote to Rufus King's 30.9 percent. Yeah, Monroe dominated, alright.

1.86% of the population voted in this election.

Turn the page for the next election, buddy.

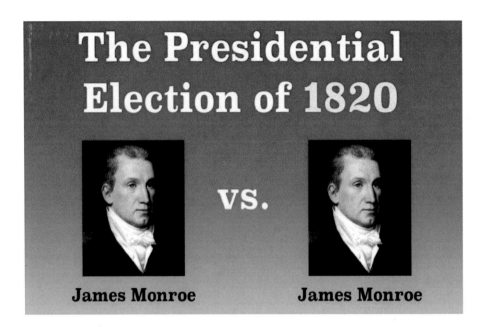

The Presidential Election of 1820

James Monroe VS. James Monroe

The ninth Presidential election in American history took place from Wednesday, November 1, to Wednesday, December 6, 1820. Oh, it was a weird one, mostly because James Monroe was so popular that everyone was too afraid to run against him. That's right, folks. This was the third and final American presidential election in history in which a candidate basically ran unopposed. Obviously, my boy George Washington ran both times unopposed.

Like I said, Monroe was extremely popular during his four years in office, a time known as "The Era of Good Feelings." However, some people were understandably upset due to the economic hard times caused by the Panic of 1819 and the rising tension between slave states and free states surrounding the passage of the Missouri Compromise.

Still, while the country did seem to divide a bit to threaten the single party system, Monroe himself was still loved by almost everyone. Since the President's renomination was never in doubt, few Democratic Republicans even bothered to show up to the nominating caucus. There was also virtually no campaigning for this election. Even former Federalists supported him. The few Federalists who remained failed to nominate a candidate. They did nominate a serious Vice President candidate named Richard Stockton, a former U.S. Senator and Representative from New Jersey. This was the last time the Federalist Party participated in a national election. The Democratic Republican Party renominated Daniel D. Tompkins for Vice President.

Four new states—Mississippi, Illinois, Alabama, and Missouri—all participated in a presidential election for the first time in 1820. However, there was a delay with Missouri because it wasn't officially a state yet at the time of the election. There had been lots of arguing in Congress, with some saying Missouri's constitution violated the United States Constitution. Nevertheless,

Missouri's electoral votes would be counted in 1820, despite not officially becoming a state until the next year.

And here are the results...

James Monroe got the win, obviously. He won all the electoral votes except one, as matter of fact. The one electoral vote against Monroe came from William Plumer, an elector and former U.S. Senator from New Hampshire. He voted for John Quincy Adams, the Secretary of State and son of former President John Adams. Why did he have to be such a nonconformist? Was it so he'd someday be given a shout out in a book like this? Well, no. Actually, he was just one of the rare folks who thought Monroe was simply not a good President. Tompkins remained the country's Vice President.

Monroe and Tompkins didn't get three of the electoral votes because those three electors originally appointed had actually died and were not replaced yet. This is why Mississippi only had two electoral votes counted, despite the fact that a state is usually always guaranteed three electoral votes.

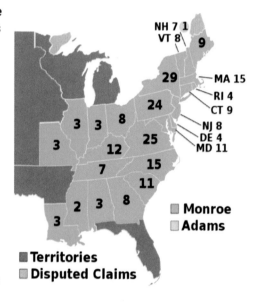

As far as the popular vote, Monroe, was....um, popular, of course, getting 80.6% of the vote. 16.1% of American voters, who were pretty much made up of the remaining Federalists, voted for "no candidate." And DeWitt Clinton, who by this time had found success as the governor of New York, still got 1.8% of the popular vote even though he didn't run for President in 1820. It's important to note that more and more states were choosing their electors by popular vote by this time.

With the country so united with who they wanted for President and Vice President in 1820, the future looked so bright.

1.34% of the population voted in this election.

Turn the page for the next election, buddy.

The Presidential Election of 1824

Henry Clay vs. William Crawford vs. John Quincy Adams vs. Andrew Jackson

The tenth Presidential election in American history took place from Tuesday, October 26, to Thursday, December 2, 1824. It's one of my favorite elections to look at because it was so unusual and fascinating. First of all, it's important to note that this was the first election in which white men came out in droves to vote. It used to be that only *rich* white men could vote in elections, but more and more laws now made it so that *poor* white men could vote because property ownership was no longer a requirement, so remember that later on.

Ok, so James Monroe had a relatively smooth tenure as President, and decided not to seek a third term, keeping the two-term tradition. His Vice President, Daniel D. Tompkins, was lucky to be reelected back in 1820 because a lot of fellow Democratic Republicans didn't like him. In 1824, he was still in no shape to run for President because many still didn't like him. He had mismanaged his money and had horrible debt, and he suffered from alcoholism and just overall poor health. Tragically, he died just three months after leaving office.

There was still only one major political party at the time–the Democratic Republican party. Yet, there was a power vacuum within the party. Because of this, a flood of candidates rushed in all wanting to be President. The election ended up being more about each candidate's personality and regional rivalries because each candidate agreed on most of the major issues. Think of the primary elections and caucuses of today within political parties to get their nominee- that's basically what this presidential election was, except they couldn't agree on who would be nominated (and later President).

There were originally six Democratic Republican candidates who stood out. However, two of them soon realized that they didn't stand much of a chance. Smith Thompson, the Secretary of the Navy from New York, quickly withdrew from the race. John Calhoun, the Secretary of War from South Carolina, withdrew soon after Thompson.

That left four other candidates who did stick it out. William H. Crawford, the U.S. Secretary of the Treasury from Georgia, had actually been nominated by a caucus of a minority of the Democratic Republican members of the U.S. Congress. However, the rest of Congress viewed the caucus as elitist and undemocratic, so they ignored it.

Next up was Henry Clay, the well-known and well-respected Speaker of the House from Kentucky. He probably would have received his party's caucus nomination if he had wanted it, but he thought the caucus process was not the best way to elect presidential candidates.

Then there was John Quincy Adams, the oldest son of former President John Adams and the U.S. Secretary of State who was from Massachusetts. Adams tended to have support from many former Federalists.

Finally, there was Andrew Jackson, the War of 1812 military hero, and also a former governor of and a current U.S. Senator from Tennessee. Many Americans tended to view Jackson as a champion of the "common man."

Like I said, with the exception of maybe disagreements over tariffs and the government's role with infrastructure, these candidates agreed on most issues- this election was about personality and supporting the candidate voters could relate to the most.

It also was very much a regional election. Crawford had much support in parts of the East, Clay had support in the West, Adams had support in the Northeast; and Jackson had support pretty much all over. Because the election was highly contested, there was heavy campaigning from all sides, with the exception of Crawford, who suffered from a stroke due to a bad prescription. However, back then candidates usually sat on the sidelines while their supporters did most of the campaigning anyway. In addition to the usual forms of campaigning, a bunch of parody songs popped up to support candidates. Most notably, there was "Hunters of Kentucky," a parody of the song "The Unfortunate Miss Bailey." Weird Al Yankovich would be so proud.

Did I mention the Vice President candidates? There were a lot. Let's see, we originally had Albert Gallatin, the former U.S. Minister to France, who was nominated by that Congressional caucus that didn't count. As it turns out, he never wanted to be Vice President anyway. Officially on the ballot in October were Nathan Sanford, a former U.S. Senator from New York, Nathaniel Macon, a U.S. Senator from North Carolina, Martin Van Buren, a U.S. Senator from New York, and the aforementioned John C. Calhoun, Henry Clay, and Andrew Jackson.

And here are the results...

Well, the results were inconclusive. Yep, there was no clear winner. Andrew Jackson received 99 electoral votes, more electoral votes than any other candidate, but he did not receive the *majority* of electoral votes needed to win the election, which was 131. John Quincy Adams came in second with 84 electoral votes, Crawford came in third with 41 electoral votes, and Clay came in fourth with 37 electoral votes.

John C. Calhoun became the seventh Vice President in American history after receiving 182 electoral votes (good thing he dropped out of the Presidential race), but who would be President? Well, the answer could be found in the Twelfth Amendment to the Constitution, which said the House of Representatives would decide who would be President if no candidate received a majority of the electoral vote.

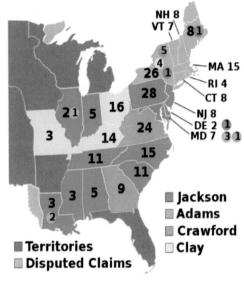

According to the Twelfth Amendment, only the top three candidates would be considered, so this left out Henry Clay. Jackson, Adams, and Crawford remained. Remember, Henry Clay was Speaker of the House, and was extremely influential in Congress. Oh, and Clay strongly disliked Andrew Jackson. In January of 1825, he told a friend, "I cannot believe that killing 2,500 Englishmen at New Orleans qualifies for the various, difficult, and complicated duties of the Chief Magistracy."

Clay used his influence to convince more people to vote for Adams, whom he agreed with more on issues anyway, instead of Jackson. When the House voted on February 9, 1825, John Quincy Adams was the winner, becoming the sixth President of the United States and the first of two Presidents who was the son of a former President, the other being George W. Bush.

Andrew Jackson and his supporters were shocked. After all, not only did Jackson receive the most electoral votes, but he received the most votes total, with 41.4% of the popular vote compared to Adams getting 30.9%. It was the first and only presidential election in which the candidate who received the most electoral votes did not become President, and the first of five presidential elections in which the candidate who won the popular vote did not become President.

After the election, word got out that Clay had struck a deal with Adams in which Clay would become Secretary of State if Adams was elected, a position Clay wanted because Adams and his three predecessors had all served as Secretary of State prior to becoming President. Sure enough, after Adams was elected, he appointed Clay to be his Secretary of State.

Jackson and his supporters were enraged, calling the apparent deal between Adams and Clay a "corrupt bargain." While Clay denied the charges, the damage was already done. The so-called "Corrupt Bargain" would haunt Adam's presidency the next four years.

26.9% of the population voted in this election, which is 13 times higher than the amount of people who voted in the previous presidential election.

Turn the page for the next election, buddy.

The Presidential Election of 1828

John Quincy Adams   vs.   Andrew Jackson

The eleventh Presidential election in American history took place from Friday, October 31, to Tuesday, December 2, 1828. It looks like we've got another rematch!

Four years prior, after a four-way split with no majority candidate, John Quincy Adams was handed the election by the House of Representatives. Andrew Jackson, who finished second in the House vote, thought the election was shady, accusing Henry Clay of a corrupt bargain to get Adams elected President so that Clay could be his Secretary of State.

Just a few months after Jackson's defeat, the Tennessee legislature already renominated him for President, setting the stage for a rematch. There was no nominating caucus even held. Jackson's supporters, who called themselves "Democrats," were rabid- they treated Jackson like a rock star. For the next three years, Jackson's support grew and grew. His supporters, also called Jacksonians, won more seats in Congress in the 1826 midterm elections.

Meanwhile, the Jacksonians criticized John Quincy Adams for seemingly everything. Their criticism peaked after Adams signed into law the Tariff of 1828, which increased tariff rates above 60 percent. Critics called it the Tariff of Abominations, as it ended up hurting the economy of several Southern states. Needless to say, a distinct shift developed- Southerners began to largely support Jackson while support for Adams was mostly only in Northern states.

President Adams was renominated by the endorsement of multiple state legislatures and partisan rallies. There was no caucus for his nomination either. Supporters of Adams called themselves National Republicans. Secretary of the Treasury Richard Rush officially ran as Adams' running mate. Wait, what the heck? Wasn't John Calhoun his Vice President? Well, yes, but Calhoun had decided to run for reelection as Jackson's running mate, interestingly enough. That traitor! Or maybe Calhoun could just see which direction the wind was blowing.

Both campaigns were incredibly nasty. Mudslinging was frequent, and Andrew Jackson was certainly an easy target. I mean, the man was involved in the slave trade, participated in the massacre of Indians, and had murdered multiple men in duels. However, things got particularly nasty when supporters of Adams started talking trash about Jackson's wife, Rachel. They even said Jackson's mom was a prostitute. People also said vicious things about Adams, saying he had surrendered an American girl to the Russian Czar when he was the Minister to Russia and that he had used public funds to buy gambling devices, which turned out to be just a chess set and a pool table.

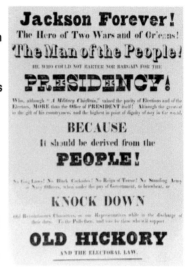

By 1828, pretty much all white men could vote, and nearly every state chose its electors through popular vote. Jackson's supporters organized a remarkable grassroot campaign that took advantage of this and brought out many first time voters. Jackson and supporter Martin Van Buren took this campaign and created the modern Democratic Party. A fitting title, as true democracy was actually becoming more of a reality.

And here are the results...

Andrew Jackson got his revenge, winning the election and becoming the seventh President of the United States. He received 178 electoral votes and won 56% of the popular vote. John Quincy Adams received 83 electoral votes, getting 43.6% of the popular vote. Adams won almost the exact same states his father did in the election of 1800.

John Calhoun was reelected Vice President, becoming the second of two vice presidents to serve under two different presidents.

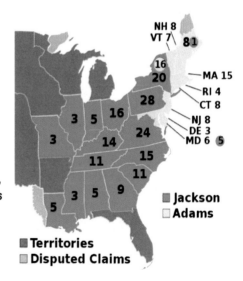

Jackson's election officially signaled a political movement toward a greater voice for the "common man," known as Jacksonian democracy. Historians also claim the election of 1828 marks the beginning of the Second Party System, as two new political parties, the Democratic Party, and the Whig Party would dominate American politics for the next 26 years.

Tragically, Rachel Jackson became ill and died shortly after the election. She had been having chest pains throughout the campaign, and was deeply upset by the personal attacks directed at her and her husband. After her death, Jackson accused the Adams campaign of causing her to die.

After the results of the election were announced, a large mob entered the White House, damaging lots of stuff in it while doing so and absolutely horrifying Adams and his staff, who just barely escaped through the back door. Large punch bowls were set up to lure the crowd back outside.

On March 4th, 1829, after Jackson was sworn in as President, Jackson again opened the White House to the public, and it turned into a crazy, huge party, with more than 20,000 people showing up. This was a perfect example of how the times had dramatically changed. John Quincy Adams had represented the old status quo- the last of the aristocratic and dignified of the Presidents. Jackson, or more appropriately Old Hickory, on the other hand, represented the new guard. This new group was largely represented by the working class. You know, the "average Joe," ready to take the country back for the masses.

57.6% of the population voted in this election, the highest ever up to that point in American history.

Turn the page for the next election, buddy.

The Presidential Election of 1832

Henry Clay vs. Andrew Jackson vs. William Wirt vs. John Floyd

The twelfth Presidential election in American history took place from Friday, November 2, to Wednesday, December 5, 1832. President Andrew Jackson, seeking reelection of course, was very popular during his first term. Well, not so popular with his Vice President, John Calhoun, who would resign shortly after the election over differences relating to tariffs that hurt his home state of South Carolina, and for several other personal reasons as well. So Jackson had to find a new Vice President to run for reelection with him, and the Democratic Party chose the dude who pretty much built the Democratic Party- Martin Van Buren, who by now was the U.S. Minister to the United Kingdom.

Sure, Jackson was popular with most Americans, but many in Congress disagreed with him on issues like his support for Indian removal, the spoils system, and getting rid of the Electoral College. The biggest issue in 1832 seemed to revolve around the renewing of the charter of the Second Bank of the United States. Congress passed it. Jackson, not a fan of central banking and paper money in general, vetoed the renewal of the Bank's charter, withdrew federal deposits from the bank, and redistributed them to private banks throughout the country. Jackson had a habit of vetoing a lot of legislation Congress passed, actually.

Needless to say, opponents of Jackson's aggressive use of veto power called him "King Andrew." They argued that not renewing the national bank would have devastating effects on the American economy. But Jackson convinced many ordinary Americans that, by being against the national bank, he was just defending them against the privileged elite who wanted to keep the power to themselves.

Jackson's opponents were led by, you guessed it, Henry Clay. Clay accepted the nomination to run against Jackson for the newly formed National Republican Party. Another name for that party could have been "The People Who Hate Andrew Jackson Party." John Sergeant, a former U.S. Representative from Pennsylvania, was Clay's running mate this time.

This was the first presidential election in American history in which a notable third party had emerged with a candidate on the ticket. The Anti-Masonic Party was created to oppose the Freemasons, who they perceived as corrupt and elitist. They called out *both* Clay and Jackson as being associated with Freemasonry. The party held the first national nominating convention in American history. Many wanted Richard Rush, the former U.S. Secretary of the Treasury, as their first nominee, but he declined. John Quincy Adams was interested, but many party leaders thought the former President was just too unpopular. The Anti-Masonic Party ended up choosing William Wirt as their presidential candidate, despite the fact he was a Freemason! Crazy! Amos Ellmaker, the former Attorney General of Pennsylvania, was his running mate. Can you tell Pennsylvania was an important state in this election?

A fourth candidate, John Floyd, the Governor of Virginia, was supported by the newly formed Nullifier Party, even though he didn't officially run for President. The Nullifier Party was basically a bunch of people in South Carolina upset about Jackson's support for increased tariffs that hurt the state.

And here are the results...

Andrew Jackson easily won reelection, receiving 219 electoral votes. He also got 54.2% of the popular vote, which is notable because no President was again able to get a majority of the popular vote in two consecutive elections until Ulysses Grant did forty years later.

Henry Clay lost yet another presidential election, coming in second place with 49 electoral votes and 37.4% of the popular vote. William Wirt received seven electoral votes and came in third place with the popular vote, at 7.8%. John Floyd received all of South Carolina's eleven electoral votes, but they didn't count the popular vote there so...that was it for John.

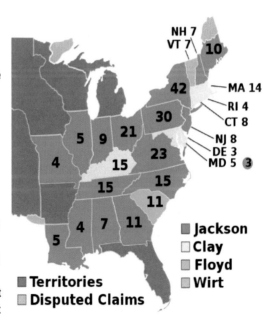

NH 7
VT 7
10
42 — MA 14
30 — RI 4
CT 8
5 9 21 NJ 8
4 15 23 DE 3
15 15 MD 5 3
11
4 7 11
5

■ Jackson
□ Clay
■ Floyd
□ Wirt
■ **Territories**
□ **Disputed Claims**

Martin Van Buren became the eighth Vice President in American history, even though all of the Democratic electors from Pennsylvania voted against him and instead voted for William Wilkins, a U.S. senator from—you guessed it—Pennsylvania.

As crazy as it sounds, Andrew Jackson would be the last president until Abraham Lincoln to be reelected. As much as some people hated him, he remained popular with many Americans.

55.4% of the population voted in this election.

Turn the page for the next election, buddy.

The Presidential Election of 1836

Martin Van Buren vs. **A Bunch of Whigs**

The thirteenth Presidential election in American history took place from Thursday, November 3, to Wednesday, December 7, 1836. Andrew Jackson? Oh, he's gone. He decided to follow in the footsteps of Washington, Jefferson, Madison, and Monroe and retire after two terms. Besides, Jackson was confident that his Vice President of the previous four years, Martin Van Buren, would do just fine in his place, especially since Van Buren shared many of his same views.

With Jackson's backing, and the fact that Van Buren helped start the Democratic Party, it was no surprise the Democratic Party nominated him. They also nominated Richard Mentor Johnson, a U.S. Representative from Kentucky, as his running mate. Johnson wasn't too popular with Southerners, however, because he had an affair with an African American woman and fathered two daughters with her.

Five years prior, a bunch of people who were disturbed by how much Andrew Jackson had expanded the power of the executive branch organized. They were led by, you guessed it, Henry Clay, a dude who constantly criticized Jackson. After they couldn't defeat Jackson in 1832, they started to gain momentum as a new political party, the Whig Party, in the years following the election. The Whig Party called for the federal government to have a more active role in the economy, which included handouts for the construction of major infrastructure projects. The Whigs also were all about protective tariffs and a national bank.

Anyway, in 1834, the Whigs began to find success in the midterm elections. By 1836, they were a major party and a major threat to Jacksonian dominance. They had a crazy strategy for this presidential election. Instead of running one candidate, like political parties usually do, they ran four different candidates in different parts of the country, hoping each would be popular enough to defeat Van Buren in each region.

The four Whig candidates were: Hugh Lawson White, a U.S. Senator from Tennessee, Willie Person Mangum, a U.S. Senator from North Carolina, Daniel Webster, a U.S. Senator from Massachusetts, and former General, U.S. Senator, U.S. Representative, and Governor, William Henry Harrison, from Ohio.

It seemed to be more about Van Buren losing than the Whigs winning. This was the only time in American history this strategy was ever tried, but no one was sure if it would work. It was certainly an experiment.

The Whigs ran two Vice President candidates. John Tyler, a U.S. Senator from Virginia, ran with White and Mangum. Francis Granger, a U.S. Representative from New York, ran with both Harrison and Webster. Those two-timers!

This was the very first election the newly formed states of Arkansas and Michigan would participate in, even though Michigan wasn't officially a state until January of the next year.

And here are the results....

First of all, there was another dispute. A lot of people didn't like the fact that Michigan's votes were counted, so the total votes were counted twice- once with Michigan, and once without it.

Either way, it didn't really matter, because Martin Van Buren won, becoming the eighth President of the United States. He received 170 electoral votes. The Whig Party's strategy backfired, as the "all or nothing" reality of the Electoral College made it so Van Buren won most of the states. In second place was William Henry Harrison, with 73 electoral votes. In third, Hugh Lawson White, with 26 electoral votes. In fourth, Daniel Webster, with 14 electoral votes. In fifth, Willie Person Mangum with eleven

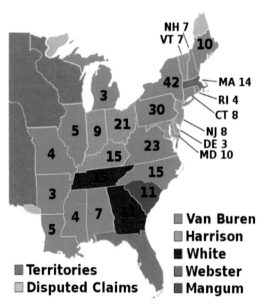

electoral votes. What the heck is with all these three name candidates, by the way? And all the U.S. Senator candidates?

Richard Mentor Johnson wasn't automatically elected Vice President. 23 faithless electors voted against him, instead voting for William Smith, a U.S. Senator from South Carolina. Another U.S. Senator, really? This left Johnson one vote short of the 148-vote majority. The Twelfth Amendment says if this happens, the Senate gets to pick. So they did, and they chose Johnson, so he became the ninth Vice President in American history. This was the only election in American history in which the Senate did this.

Just looking at the popular vote in terms of political parties, it was much closer. Van Buren got 50.8% of the popular vote compared to the nearly 50% all the Whig candidates got combined.

The presidential election of 1836 was the last one until 1988 to result in a Vice President becoming promoted, for lack of a better word, to President, through election. Some others would do so because the President died or resigned, but not through straight up election. Pretty crazy, right?

57.8% of the population voted in this election.

Turn the page for the next election, buddy.

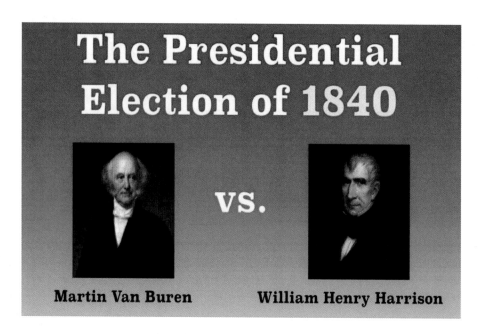

The Presidential Election of 1840

vs.

Martin Van Buren   **William Henry Harrison**

The fourteenth Presidential election in American history took place from Friday, October 30, to Wednesday, December 2, 1840. Martin Van Buren fought for reelection during a time when the economy was not doing so well. Well that's never an easy thing. Yep, the country was in the middle of a horrible recession, which began as a financial crisis referred to as the Panic of 1837. Due to this, President Van Buren was unpopular. But you know who was more unpopular? His Vice President, Richard Mentor Johnson. The Democratic Party actually refused to renominate him. In fact, they didn't officially nominate anybody, although many wanted James Polk, the Governor of Tennessee, or Littleton Tazewell, the former Governor of Virginia.

The Whig Party, meanwhile, was gaining strength, and learned their lesson from the last election, this time uniting behind just one candidate for President- William Henry Harrison. Not only was Harrison a well established politician, but, like Andrew Jackson, he was a bit of a war hero. Harrison's running mate was John Tyler, a former U.S. Senator from Virginia.

Harrison was the first candidate in American history to actively campaign to be President. His supporters came up with a pretty catchy slogan- "Tippecanoe and Tyler too." Get it? Of course you don't. Well basically, Tippecanoe referred to Harrison's military victory over the Shawnee American Indians on November 7, 1811 at the Battle of Tippecanoe. Because of this, the Whigs aggressively organized to promote him as a war hero.

But the Democrats argued that Harrison was too old to be President. Many called him "Granny," implying that maybe he was senile. The Whigs fought back by portraying Martin Van Buren as a rich snob, out of touch with most Americans, and Harrison as a man of the common people from the Western frontier. In reality, it was Harrison who was richer than Van Buren, but most Americans wouldn't know that by the campaign.

The election of 1840 was more about image and less about substance. In fact, the Whigs were just fine if Harrison didn't argue policy or about issues, because the country was pretty divided at the time. Instead, the Whig strategy was to avoid difficult national issues such as the expansion of slavery out west and instead focus on how the Van Buren administration ruined the economy.

Speaking of slavery, one notable third party, the Liberty Party, sprung up in 1840 with its primary goal to end slavery. They ran a well-known abolitionist named James Birney for President and the lesser known abolitionist Thomas Earle as his running mate.

Interestingly enough, the Anti-Masonic Party also nominated William Henry Harrison for President, but with the legendary Massachusetts U.S. Senator Daniel Webster as his running mate instead of Tyler.

And here are the results...

William Henry Harrison won, becoming the ninth President of the United States. He received 234 electoral votes and won 52.9% of the popular vote. As matter of fact, 42.4% of all eligible voters voted for him, the highest percentage in American history up to that time.

Martin Van Buren finished second, receiving 60 electoral votes but 46.8% of the popular vote. Van Buren was so unpopular he even lost in his home state of New York, which rarely happens for a Presidential candidate. James Birney received .3% of the popular vote, which proved the nation wasn't ready to end slavery yet.

The election was special because it was the only one in which electors cast votes for four different men who had been or would become President. Van Buren, Harrison, John Tyler, who became the tenth Vice President in American history, and future President James

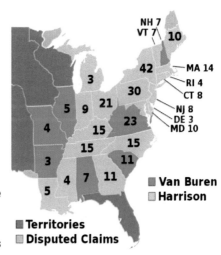

Polk. Oops, I forgot to say spoiler alert! Yeah Polk got one electoral vote for Vice President. Tazewell got eleven, and Johnson apparently was still popular enough to get 48.

67-year old Harrison was the oldest President elected in American history up until Ronald Reagan was elected in 1980.

After Harrison was sworn in as President, he gave the longest inauguration speech in American history, at about 1 hour, 45 minutes and 8,445 words. Although the weather was cool, he refused to wear a jacket. The common myth is that this caused him to catch a cold, which later turned into pneumonia and die. Well, he did catch a cold that turned into pneumonia and died, but he didn't catch the cold until more than three weeks later, so him not wearing a jacket at his inauguration speech is totally unrelated. Harrison died on April 4, 1841, making his 32 days in office the shortest tenure in history. Because Harrison was the first President to die while in office, there was some confusion as to how to carry on next.

The Constitution said:
"In Case of the Removal of the President from Office, or of his Death, Resignation, or Inability to discharge the Powers and Duties of the said Office, the same shall devolve on the Vice President."

So what does that mean? Well, John Tyler pretty much interpreted it as "I'm President now, fools, so whatcha gonna do, huh?"

80.2% of the population voted in this election.

Turn the page for the next election, buddy.

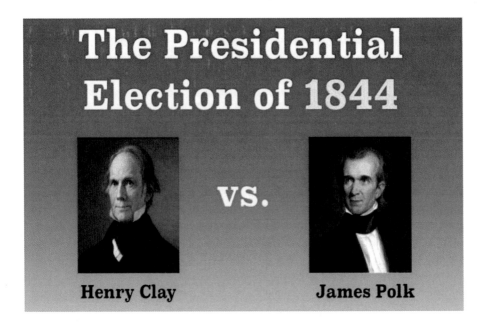

The Presidential Election of 1844

Henry Clay   vs.   **James Polk**

The fifteenth Presidential election in American history took place from Friday, November 1, to Wednesday, December 4, 1844. This was the last presidential election to be held on different days in different states. All future presidential elections would be held on a single day.

President John Tyler had taken over after William Henry Harrison died, but he remained at odds with the Whig Party. The Whig Party actually stopped supporting him, and so did the Democratic Party, his old party. At odds with both of the major political parties in the country, he tried to start a third party movement for reelection, hoping that many who agreed with him on the annexation of Texas would support him.

The Texas annexation issue would divide not only the country but the Democratic Party. Martin Van Buren, originally a shoe-in for the Democratic nomination in 1844, was against the annexation of Texas. However, many influential southern Democrats, like U.S. Secretary of State John Calhoun and former President Andrew Jackson, wanted Texas. At the Democratic National Convention, three nominees were discussed at first- Van Buren, James Buchanan, a U.S. Senator from Pennsylvania, and Lewis Cass, the Ambassador to France. Then, seemingly out of nowhere, came James Polk, a former governor of Tennessee and former Speaker of the House. Though Polk had originally entered the convention hoping to be the Vice President nominee, by the end of the convention he was the most popular guy in the room, getting the nomination unanimously. Polk famously became the first well-known "dark horse" candidate, meaning before the election he was not well known. George Dallas, a former U.S. Senator from Pennsylvania, was nominated as Polk's running mate. The fact that the city of Dallas, Texas was probably named after him might be a hint as to who would win the election.

The Whig Party was firmly against Texas annexation. After abandoning John Tyler, the party went back to the original Whig- Henry Clay, the former U.S. Senator representing Kentucky who was pretty much the leading Whig ever since the party began. Though Clay had run before for President and lost many times before, things seemed to be going more his way this time, as he could appeal to both Southern slave owners who didn't want to annex Texas because it might make their land less valuable and slaves more expensive, and Northerners who didn't want slavery to expand further west. In 1840, the Whigs did quite well with Harrison, and with Clay, they just assumed it would be another blowout. The Whigs nominated Theodore Frelinghuysen, a former U.S. Senator from New Jersey, as Clay's running mate.

Things got a little more complicated when John Tyler dropped out of the running for re-election and threw his support to Polk. Also, the abolitionist Liberty Party ran the activist James Birney again with former U.S. Senator Thomas Morris, who was from Ohio, as his running mate. Birney's support had grown since 1840, and some worried that Northern Whigs might vote for him instead of Clay.

So though Clay was confident he would win at first, as the election drew nearer, Polk's support had grown. Polk was all about Manifest Destiny, or the belief that it was the United States' destiny to expand from the Atlantic Ocean to the Pacific Ocean. Polk wanted to expand the country's border whenever and wherever possible, and more and more Americans seemed to agree with him. Polk called for not only adding Texas, but also California and Oregon territory. The northern boundary of Oregon, which Britain claimed as well, was the latitude line of 54 degrees, 50 minutes. Many of his extremist supporters used the slogan "54° 40' or Fight!" in hopes that a Polk presidency meant getting all of Oregon.

And here are the results...

Manifest Destiny was proving to be pretty popular, so ultimately that was why James Polk won, narrowly defeating Henry Clay to become the eleventh President of the United States. Polk received 170 electoral votes. Clay received 105 electoral votes, although the popular vote was much closer, with Polk getting 49.5% of the popular vote and Clay getting 48.1%. 20% more Democrats came out and voted in this election compared to the 1840 election, while only 4% more Whigs came out.

James Birney received 2.3% of the popular vote, a much better showing than the 1840 election.

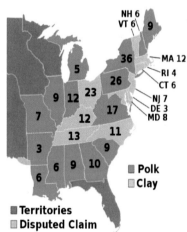

George Dallas became the eleventh Vice President in American history.

This was the only presidential election in which both major party nominees were former Speakers of the House.

At age 49, James Polk was the youngest to become President up to that point in American history. Polk promised to serve only one term, and he went straight to work. Within a little over one year in office, Polk would get half of Oregon and be at war with Mexico over Texas after its annexation.

78.9% of the population voted in this election.

Turn the page for the next election, buddy.

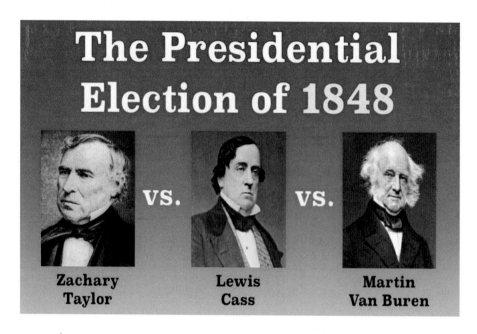

The Presidential Election of 1848

Zachary Taylor vs. **Lewis Cass** vs. **Martin Van Buren**

The sixteenth Presidential election in American history took place on Tuesday, November 7th, 1848. This was the first election that took place on the same day in every state. By law from this point forward, Election Day would be on a Tuesday.

James Polk had one of the most productive presidential terms in American history . Every major objective he had going into office was accomplished. He had got half of Oregon without going to war with Britain, got the northern half of Mexico by bullying them into a war, reduced tariffs, and created an independent treasury. Satisfied with accomplishing his goals, he promised not to run for re-election. His health was actually declining anyway, and he would die of cholera three months after leaving office, having the shortest retirement of all Presidents in American history.

In his place, the Democratic Party nominated Lewis Cass, who since 1844 had become a U.S. Senator for Michigan. Cass beat out Martin Van Buren for the nomination, who was no longer having luck with the political party he helped create. The Democrats nominated William Orlando Butler to run with Cass, a former U.S. Representative from Kentucky and a general who had recently fought in the Mexican American War.

Martin Van Buren, upset and perhaps bitter at losing to Cass for the nomination, found a new political party. That new party was the Free Soil Party, led by abolitionist Salmon P. Chase and John Parker Hale, a U.S. Senator from New Hampshire. Mostly based out of New York, the party called for ending the expansion of slavery out west. Most of their support came from anti-slavery Democrats, but some Whigs also joined their cause. They indeed chose Van Buren their nominee, with Charles Francis Adams, a son of John Quincy Adams and a grandson of John Adams, as his running mate.

Partially because of the rise of the Free Soil Party, the Liberty Party lost most of its support. They did nominate Gerrit Smith, brother-in-law to their former presidential nominee, James Birney. Keep it in the family! Smith's running mate was Charles Foote, a minister from Michigan.

What about the Whigs? Well, General Zachary Taylor, of Louisiana, was an attractive candidate because he was a war hero, leading American forces to key victories in the Mexican American War. Here's the thing, though. He wasn't very political, and had never even voted in an election himself. In fact, this is why Taylor was courted by both the Whig Party and the Democratic Party- few knew exactly where he even stood on major issues.

Taylor decided to declare himself as a Whig, though, and easily won their nomination, beating out big names like Henry Clay, Daniel Webster, and fellow Mexican American war hero Winfield Scott. Millard Fillmore, a former U.S. Representative and the Comptroller of New York, was Taylor's running mate.

The campaigns were pretty chill this time, with no major issues that sharply divided the parties. I say that because the Free Soil Party had a small chance of actually winning because they weren't on the ballot in several states. In the early part of the Mexican American War, the Whigs mostly criticized James Polk for his recklessness that led to the war. However, after the United States kicked butt in the war, now the Whigs had seemed to forget this, and were glorifying General Taylor's war success. Taylor himself was pretty vague about where he stood on the issues, though.

GRAND PRESIDENTIAL SWEEP-STAKES FOR 1848.

This was the first election in which citizens of the new states of Florida, Texas, Iowa, and Wisconsin could all cast votes.

And here are the results...

Zachary Taylor won, becoming the twelfth President of the United States. This was the Whig Party's second and last Presidential win, but they would remain a big force for several years. Taylor received 163 electoral votes. Lewis Cass received 127 electoral votes. Martin Van Buren and Gerrit Smith didn't receive any electoral votes. Taylor received 47.3% of the popular vote to Cass's 42.5%, Van Buren's 10.1%, and Smith's .1%.

Millard Fillmore became the twelfth Vice President in American history.

This was the first of two presidential elections where the two leading candidates evenly split the states for the electoral vote. Historian George Pierce Garrison later wrote of this election: "Practically the only thing it decided was that a Whig general should be made President because he had done effective work in carrying on a Democratic war."

Had Taylor ran as a Democrat, he likely still would have won the election, so the Whigs lucked out by getting him.

72.7% of the population voted in this election.

Turn the page for the next election, buddy.

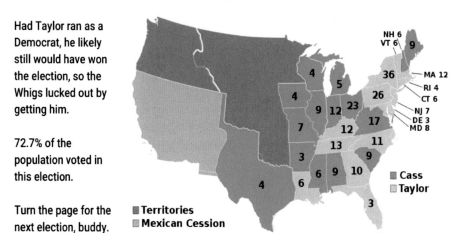

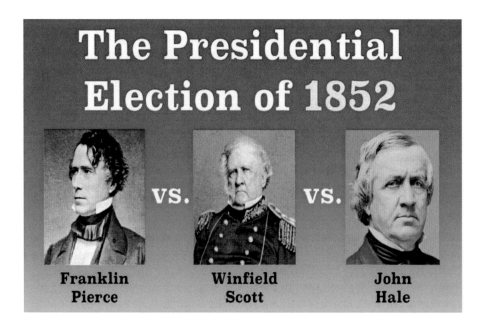

The Presidential Election of 1852

Franklin Pierce   vs.   Winfield Scott   vs.   John Hale

The seventeenth Presidential election in American history took place on November 2nd, 1852. You might call this election the election of 1844: Part 2, because it was very similar to it. Just like in 1844, a young dark horse candidate won. Also like in 1844, the incumbent president was a Whig who had become President after the death of his war-hero predecessor. Additionally, that Whig didn't get his party's nomination for the next election.

In 1852, the Whig was Millard Fillmore, who took over after Zachary Taylor died in 1850. The biggest national issue during Taylor and Fillmore's presidencies was the expansion of slavery out in western territories. The Compromise of 1850 had helped ease tensions a bit, but it really just kicked the can down the road- the country was becoming further divided between Northerners and Southerners over slavery.

You know who else was divided? The Whig Party. They had a hard time deciding who their nominee for the 1852 election would be. Many favored Fillmore, but many others favored Mexican American War hero Winfield Scott. Yep, Old Fuss and Feathers himself. Even others favored Secretary of State Daniel Webster. In the end, it was Scott who would get the nomination. William Alexander Graham, the Secretary of the Navy and former governor and U.S. Senator from North Carolina, was his running mate.

The Democratic Party had at least nine candidates who were all fighting to get nominated. At their convention, four major candidates stood out. Lewis Cass, the U.S. Senator from Michigan who won the nomination in 1848, James Buchanan, the former Secretary of State and U.S.

Senator from Pennsylvania, Stephen Douglas, a U.S. Senator from Illinois, and William L. Marcy, the former Secretary of War. Then, seemingly out of nowhere, comes another dark horse candidate for the Democrats- Franklin Pierce, a 48 year-old former U.S. Senator and U.S. Representative from New Hampshire. They ended up nominating Pierce, with William R. King, a former U.S. Senator and U.S. Representative from Alabama, as his running mate. A Northerner and Southerner running together? Hey, smart move.

There were plenty of third parties in this election. The biggest was the Free Soil Party, which had a strong showing in 1848. They nominated John P. Hale, another U.S. Senator from New Hampshire, with George Washington Julian as his running mate. Julian was a U.S. Representative from Indiana who was later a Radical Republican before it was cool.

The Union Party formed after many Whigs were upset with Winfield Scott's nomination. They nominated Daniel Webster, the legendary U.S. Senator from Massachusetts, for President.

Then there was the Native American Party, but it's probably not the type of "Native American" you are thinking of. They were a nativist party, favoring citizens born in the country before immigrants. The Native American Party was also called the Know-Nothing Party by opponents who thought they...well...knew nothing. Surprisingly, the party embraced the nickname because I guess they liked being called stupid. They also nominated Daniel Webster, even though he didn't approve.

Finally, there was the Southern Rights Party, an offshoot of the Democratic Party that nominated George Troup, a former U.S. Senator and U.S. Representative from Georgia who also was governor of the state.

This was the first election in which citizens of the new state of California could vote. The two biggest political parties- the Whigs and the Democrats, had similar platforms, so the campaigns were mostly just about the personalities of Pierce and Scott. This jaded a lot of voters and explains why so many third parties popped up. The lack of clear-cut issues would cause the voter turnout to decline.

And here are the results...

Franklin Pierce won in a landslide, becoming the fourteenth President of the United States. Oh, Pierce dominated, alright. He received 254 electoral votes, and Winfield Scott only received 42 electoral votes. Pierce received 50.8% of the popular vote and Scott received just 43.9%. John P. Hale came in third, with 4.9% of the popular vote. All other candidates received much less than 1% of the popular vote.

Daniel Webster, the Union Party and unofficial Native American Party candidate, died one week before the election. Despite this, he got 7,000 votes and finished fourth in the election. The fact that this many people voted for him even though he was dead sort of proves how disappointed voters were with the two biggest candidates.

William R. King became the thirteenth Vice President in American history. He died six weeks after taking office, serving the shortest tenure in history in that position for someone who didn't later become President.

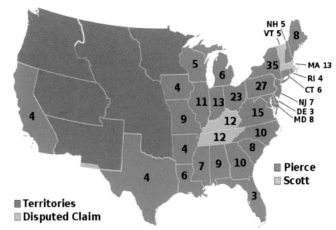

Baby-face Pierce became the youngest President in American history up to that point. Tragedy seemed to follow this guy around a lot. Before he was even sworn into office, he was in a train accident which killed his only surviving son. This cast a great shadow on his Presidency, which most historians say did not go well.

Scott losing the election of 1852 was devastating for the Whigs, and the election was the last one in which they even ran a candidate. Following the election, the party began to collapse.

69.6% of the population voted in this election.

Turn the page for the next election, buddy.

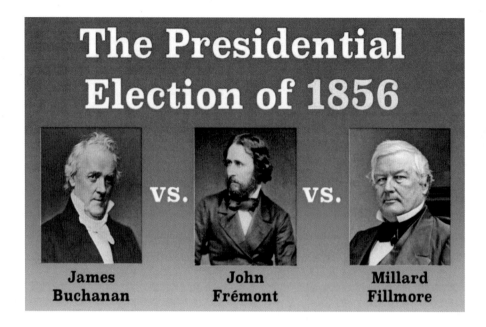

The Presidential Election of 1856

VS.   **VS.**

James Buchanan   **John Frémont**   **Millard Fillmore**

The eighteenth Presidential election in American history took place on November 4th, 1856.

Franklin Pierce had a rough time over the previous four years, and now struggled to get his own party's renomination. At the Democratic Party's convention, four main candidates were in the running: Pierce, James Buchanan, who was now the U.S. Minister to the United Kingdom, Little Giant himself Stephen Douglas, the U.S. Senator from Illinois, and the beautiful Lewis Cass, who was still a U.S. Senator for Michigan. It was a tight race between four well-established and qualified candidates. In the end, Buchanan won the nomination. His running mate was John C. Breckinridge, a former U.S. Representative from Kentucky.

By this time, the Whig Party had mostly collapsed. Most former Whigs had joined either the Know Nothing Party or a brand new political party called the Republican Party.

The Republican Party was formed in 1854 to oppose the extremely controversial Kansas Nebraska Act. At the first Republican National Convention in June 1856, they met to approve an anti-slavery platform, an end to polygamy in Mormon settlements, and federal aid for a transcontinental railroad. Their nominee for President was John C. Fremont, a former U.S. Senator, explorer, and simply world's most interesting man from California, although Supreme Court justice John McClean from Ohio was in the running. Fremont's running mate was William L. Dayton, a former U.S. Senator from New Jersey.

The American Party, formerly the Native American Party and nicknamed the "Know Nothing Party," by this time had gained much support for their nativist platform. Nativism is the policy of protecting the interests native citizens against foreigners, and the American Party mostly targeted Irish Catholics, who they complained were hurting the country. Even though former President Millard Fillmore was not a member of the American Party, nor was he a nativist, nor did he ever attend an American Party function, the party nominated him to be President again. He was actually out of the country at the time of the nomination, and had not been consulted beforehand. Still, he just sort of went with it. The Know-Nothings nominated Andrew Jackson Donelson, the nephew of Andrew Jackson.

There were two other political parties that ran candidates for President. They were the deceptively named North American Party and the North American Seceders Party, but they were pretty insignificant so we won't go into who they endorsed.

Slavery was the inescapable issue of the day, and it would be quite an understatement to say the country was divided on the issue. The Republican Party unapologetically opposed expanding slavery out west. It's slogan was "Free speech, free press, free soil, free men, Fremont, and victory!" The Democrats warned that a Fremont victory would bring a civil war.
The American Party attacked Fremont also, calling him a....*gasp*...a Catholic, even though it wasn't true. He was likely an Episcopalian.

COL. FREMONT
PLANTING THE AMERICAN STANDARD ON THE ROCKY MOUNTAINS.

The fact is, despite their xenophobia, the American Party attracted many who were scared at how divided the country had become. Their candidate, Fillmore, promised a return to unity, attempting to fulfill the role of the moderate.

And here are the results...

James Buchanan won, becoming the fifteenth President of the United States, despite not receiving a majority of the vote. He received 174 electoral votes and 45.3% of the popular vote. John C. Fremont finished pretty strongly for a new political party. He

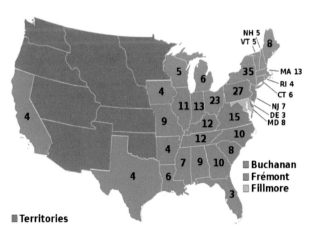

received 114 electoral votes and 33.1% of the popular vote.

Millard Fillmore came in third, receiving eight electoral votes–which was just the state of Maryland–and 21.5% of the popular vote.

John C. Breckinridge became the fourteenth Vice President in American history.

This presidential election was the only time in American history in which a political party stopped a renomination of the incumbent and still ended up winning.

The success of the Republican Party was troublesome for many southerners. After this election, the country seemed to be just hanging on, trying desperately to stay unified. By the next presidential election, secession was much more of a reality than just a talking point.

78.9% of the population voted in this election.

Turn the page for the next election, buddy.

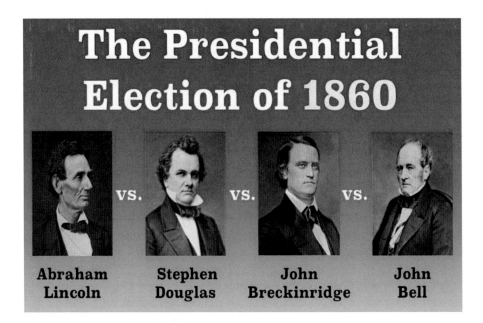

The Presidential Election of 1860

Abraham Lincoln **vs.** Stephen Douglas **vs.** John Breckinridge **vs.** John Bell

Who knew that a Presidential election could directly lead to war? The nineteenth Presidential election in American history took place on November 6th, 1860, exactly 121 years before the day I was born. This presidential election was a big freaking deal. As I wrote before, the United States had been growing more divided throughout the 1850s over the issue of the expansion of slavery out west and the rights of slave owners.

In 1860, tensions were obviously high, not only between Democrats and Republicans, but within the Democratic Party. At the Democratic National Conventions, extreme pro-slavery "Fire-eaters," walked out in protest. They were nicknamed "Fire-eaters" because they refused to compromise on slavery to a point where they wanted to secede and start their own country. They ended up being known as the Southern Democratic Party, as most of them were Southerners, and nominated their own candidates. Those who remained in the Democratic Party nominated Stephen Douglas, who by this time was very well known across the country as a moderate on the slavery issue who favored "popular sovereignty" to resolve the conflict. Benjamin Fitzpatrick, a U.S. Senator from Alabama, was nominated for Vice President, but he refused the nomination, so they nominated Herschel Johnson, the former Governor of Georgia, instead. So both were the nominees for what became known as the Northern Democratic Party.

Meanwhile, the Southern Democratic Party got together again and nominated current Vice President John C. Breckinridge for President and Joseph Lane, a U.S. Senator from Oregon, as his running mate. Wait, Oregon? Oregon's a state now? Heck yeah. Both Oregon and Minnesota were now states, and got to participate in this election for the first time.

Oh yeah, James Buchanan, the current President, wasn't even brought up as a nominee for reelection. That shows you just how unpopular he was. Remember, he was a Democrat, but apparently both Southern and Northern Democrats were united over their hatred of him.

The Republican Party, now stronger than they were in 1856, had four top contenders for their nomination. William Seward, a U.S. Senator from New York, Salmon P. Chase, a former governor and U.S. Senator of Ohio, Edward Bates, a former U.S. Representative from Missouri, and rising star Abraham Lincoln, a former U.S. Representative from Illinois. Lincoln had become famous after a series of highly publicized debates with Stephen Douglas when the two both ran for the U.S. Senate in Illinois in 1858. Lincoln had lost that election, but now had a chance to face his old rival again, this time for a much higher office.

You might already know this, but Lincoln won the nomination, mostly because he was the most moderate of the four I mentioned. The Republicans chose Hannibal Hamlin, a U.S. Senator from Maine, as his running mate.

To further complicate this election, there were other nominees. Former Whigs who wanted to avoid the country splitting up over the slavery issue created a new political party called the Constitutional Union Party. Their slogan was: "The Union as it is, and the Constitution as it is." So yeah, I guess the name fit. They nominated John Bell, a former U.S. Senator from Tennessee, with Edward Everett, a really charismatic speaker and former Governor and U.S. Senator of Massachusetts, as his running mate.

There were other candidates, but in a crowded field already, the other candidates barely had any support, so I will not mention them here. It seemed to be another classic four-way race.

While Lincoln and the Republicans promised they did not want to ban slavery completely, many Southerners weren't convinced, and swore if Lincoln won, then they were gone. Meaning, they would call for their states to secede. In other words, if Lincoln won they would break away from the United States and start their own country. In ten southern states, Lincoln wasn't even on the ballot. While the Northern Democrats and Constitutional Union Party campaigned like they were the ones who could keep the country united, both ironically further caused the country to divide, as we will soon find out.

Stephen Douglas made numerous personal appearances and gave speeches to campaign, which was rare at the time. In fact, Douglas changed the game by doing this, and many more later would follow in his path. This election also had campaign fliers with photographs of the candidates for the first time. Imagine that. Americans, for the first time, could finally see what the candidates actually looked like.

Voters came out to the polls in higher numbers more so than at any point prior in American history. It's an understatement to say the stakes were high.

And here are the results....

Although he won less than 40% of the popular vote, Abraham Lincoln won, becoming the sixteenth President of the United States. While this election had the second-highest voter turnout in American history, it was very sectional. For example, the three states with the highest voter turnouts voted the most one-sided.

Looking at this map you can easily tell how if you lived in a certain part of the country, chances are you were voting for the same candidate as your region or state:

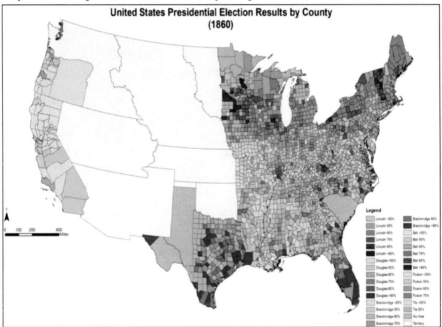

The South was a little less united than the North in who they voted for, though.

Abraham Lincoln, who today is considered by most historians to be the best American President in history, in 1860 only had support of mostly Northerners. He did receive an impressive 180 electoral votes, though, as the North had most of the population of the country.

Hannibal Hamlin became the fifteenth Vice President in American history.

John C. Breckinridge finished second in the Electoral College, receiving 72 electoral votes, but third in the popular vote, with 18.1%. John Bell finished third in the Electoral College, receiving 39 electoral votes, but fourth in the popular vote, with 12.6%. Stephen Douglas finished fourth in the Electoral College, receiving 12 electoral votes, but was 2nd in the popular vote, with 29.5%. Douglas was the only candidate winning electoral votes in both slave and free states, winning free state New Jersey and slave state Missouri.

How much did the South hate Lincoln? In the one southern state where he was on the ballot, he received just 1.1% of the popular vote.

This election was a direct cause of southern states beginning to secede from the Union. Immediately following the election results, a South Carolina convention declared "that the Union now subsisting between South Carolina and other states under the name of 'United States of America' is hereby dissolved." It was the first state to leave. By the time Abraham Lincoln was inaugurated, six more Southern states would follow, forming a new country called the Confederate States of America.

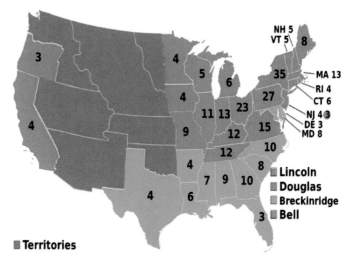

Lincoln, of course, was against secession, and did not recognize the new country. On April 12, 1861, after a group of pro-Union forces refused to abandon their post at Fort Sumter in South Carolina, Confederate forces attacked and easily took them over. This was the beginning of the American Civil War. Just five weeks after being sworn in, Lincoln found himself fighting in what would become, by far, the deadliest war in American history. Welcome to the Presidency, Mr. Lincoln!

81.2% of the population voted in this election.

Turn the page for the next election, buddy.

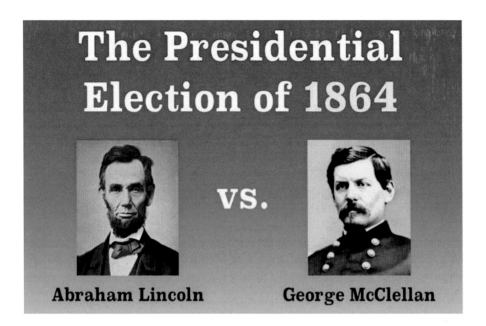

The Presidential Election of 1864

VS.

Abraham Lincoln　　　　**George McClellan**

Who cares if the southern half of the country split off and it's been fighting a very bloody war against it ever since? Let's have an election! The twentieth Presidential election in American history took place on November 8th, 1864, which was right smack dab during the Civil War, so yeah, Americans were a bit...preoccupied.

By the summer of 1864, the North (aka the Union) had gained momentum. The South (aka the Confederate States of America) was retreating, yet were not showing signs of giving up. Hundreds of thousands had already died. Even though the Union won the Battle of Gettysburg and the Siege of Vicksburg the previous summer, they had lost over 65,000 soldiers to do it. In comparison, they had lost 108,000 during the entire war up to that point.

Many Northerners were growing tired of the war. Some who originally were excited about the war now questioned the point of it. They were also questioning the President himself, the man who led them into it- Abraham Lincoln.

Lincoln was questioning his ability to get reelected, and rightly so. The country hadn't reelected a President since Andrew Jackson 32 years prior, way back in 1832. Lincoln had made many enemies, especially in Congress. He now openly embraced the emancipation of all slaves, and even Northerners turned against him because of this. Lincoln's suspension of the writ of habeas corpus was ruled unconstitutional by the Supreme Court. Obviously, this war had been a nightmare, and the stress had aged him considerably.

Two distinct factions developed in both the Republican Party and the Democratic Party.

First, some Republicans who didn't like Lincoln split off. They called themselves "Radical Republicans," and formed a new political party called the Radical Democracy Party. Woah...what a radical name. The radicals nominated John C. Fremont for President and general John Cochrane for Vice President, but their plan backfired as Fremont later ended up backing Lincoln after he was afraid the Democrats might win. More on the Democrats in a bit.

Lincoln and other Republicans formed a new political party as well, called the National Union Party. Some Democrats even joined. They had a clear, impressively specific platform. They wanted "pursuit of the war until the Confederacy surrendered unconditionally; a constitutional amendment for the abolition of slavery; aid to disabled Union veterans; continued European neutrality; enforcement of the Monroe Doctrine; encouragement of immigration; and construction of a transcontinental railroad."

Lincoln wanted to go with a new running mate this time, dropping Hannibal Hamlin to broaden his support. He went with a Democrat. That's right, a Democrat! The National Union Party nominated Andrew Johnson, a former U.S. Senator and current Military Governor of Tennessee for Vice President.

Fortunately for the Republicans, the Democratic Party was even more split than them. The two major factions were the War Democrats and Peace Democrats. Extreme War Democrats wanted to finish the job completely. Extreme Peace Democrats, nicknamed Copperheads, wanted to stop the war immediately. Looking for unity, they nominated George McClellan, the general that Lincoln had fired two years before. McClellan was definitely a War Democrat, but he was very popular, and the Democrats nominated the Peace Democrat George Pendleton, a U.S. Representative from Ohio, for Vice President to balance it out. Though McClellan personally was for continuing the war, the two ran a campaign for ending the war, so basically a peace platform.

The fact that the Democrats were split and with Fremont changing his mind to endorse him gave Lincoln confidence he could actually get reelected. Lincoln probably gained more confidence when on September 6, 1864, General William Tecumseh Sherman led forces to take over Atlanta and his March to the Sea thereafter devastated the South.

So it was basically McClellan versus Lincoln, with McClellan getting the opportunity for payback. Only 25 states participated in this election, since 11 Southern states had left the country to form the Confederacy. However, three new states participated for the first time- my home state of Kansas, West Virginia, and Nevada.

And here are the results...

Well you probably already know this, but Abraham Lincoln won. It was a landslide. Lincoln received 212 electoral votes, and 55% of the popular vote.

Andrew Johnson became the sixteenth Vice President in American history.

George McClellan received 21 electoral votes and 45% of the popular vote. He won just three states- Kentucky, Delaware, and his home state of New Jersey.

Lincoln was the first incumbent President reelected since Andrew Jackson. By the time he was inaugurated, on March 4, 1865, the Union forces were closing in on Confederate leader Robert E. Lee. Things were looking good for the Union. However, Lincoln tragically became the first American President to be assassinated just five weeks later.

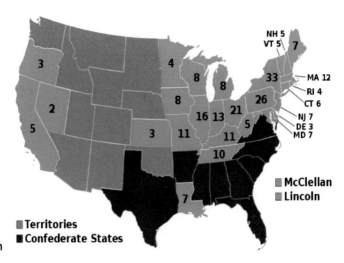

But the Civil War ended soon after, and though Lincoln didn't live to see it, one main goal of his entire Presidency was to preserve the Union, and that he did. That he did.

73.8% of the population voted in this election.

Turn the page for the next election, buddy.

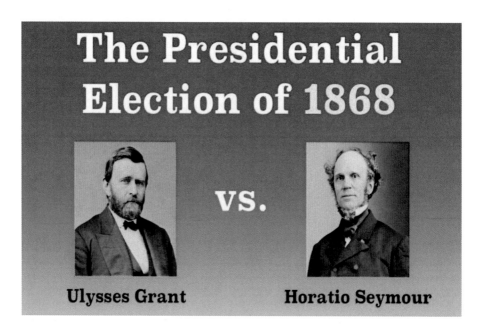

The Presidential Election of 1868

vs.

Ulysses Grant

Horatio Seymour

The twenty-first Presidential election in American history took place on November 3rd, 1868. It was the first one to take place after the Civil War, and the first to take place during a period historians refer to as the Reconstruction Era. The country was still healing. The wounds were still fresh. Three of the former Confederate states—Texas, Mississippi, and Virginia—hadn't even yet been officially brought back into the Union.

Andrew Johnson had taken over as President after Abraham Lincoln was assassinated. Now, he didn't even get renominated by the Democratic Party. He had managed to make a lot of people mad during his Presidency, especially the Radical Republicans, who favored a stricter Reconstruction policy which punished former Confederate leaders and equal rights for African Americans.

Every time Johnson vetoed one of their Reconstruction bills, they overrode his vetoes, more so than any other Congress in history. Things got ugly. In fact, Johnson was the first President ever impeached, for breaking the Office of Tenure Act. Although he wasn't kicked out of office—by just one vote I might add—his reputation was badly hurt after this. So yeah, the Democratic Party went quickly looking for someone else.

They found Horatio Seymour, who absolutely did not want to be the nominee. Seriously, it was crazy. I have never seen someone so badly not want the nomination actually get it. Seymour was the former governor of New York, and was the Democratic Party convention chairman. He repeatedly and vocally told everyone there he didn't want the nomination, but everyone there couldn't passionately get behind someone other than Seymour. After lots of pressure, he finally accepted. The Democrats nominated Francis Blair, a former U.S. Representative and Civil War general from Missouri, for Vice President. Blair was extraordinarily racist, by the way, giving dramatic speeches about how African American men always got into trouble.

Meanwhile, the Union Party was once again the Republican Party. It was important for the party to nominate a popular Civil War hero as their candidate. Fortunately, General Ulysses Grant, who just so happened to be the hero who helped the North win the Civil War, announced to everyone he was a Republican. He was unanimously nominated on the first ballot. The Republicans nominated Schuyler Colfax, the Speaker of the House, for Vice President. Colfax, who represented Indiana, was one of those Radical Republicans I mentioned earlier that clashed with Andrew Johnson.

It had appeared it would be a close race. In Grant's letter of acceptance, he said "let us have peace." That ended up becoming sort of a slogan for his campaign. The Radical Republicans ended up being loudest on the campaign trail, even though Grant was certainly not one himself. Seymour ran on a platform calling for the repayment of the war debt in greenbacks, a form of currency not backed by gold or silver.

The campaigns turned a bit vicious. Grant supporters said Seymour would probably commit suicide because his dad did. Seymour supporters said Grant was a drunk.

Since the last election, Nebraska had been admitted to the Union, so they got to participate in a presidential election for the first time. Yay for them.

And here are the results...

Ulysses Grant won, becoming the eighteenth President in American history. He dominated with electoral votes, getting 214 compared to Seymour getting 80. However, the popular vote was much closer. Grant won 52.7% of the popular vote and Seymour got 47.3%.

Schuyler Colfax became the seventeenth Vice President in American history.

Many Republicans were surprised at how close the vote actually was.

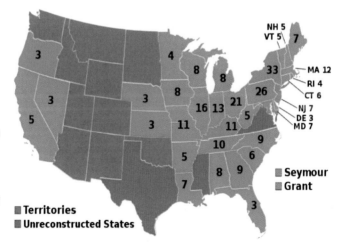

Republicans counted on getting the immigrant vote, as most immigrants were Northerners, but many ended up voting for Seymour instead. While Republicans would dominate the Presidency into the next century, this election was a sign of things to come- the Democrats weren't going away any time soon, and would consistently be a threat.

78.1% of the population voted in this election.

Turn the page for the next election, buddy.

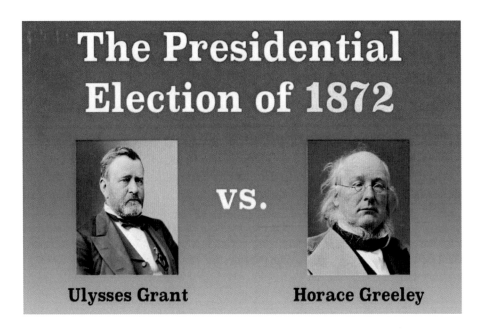

The Presidential Election of 1872

VS.

Ulysses Grant   **Horace Greeley**

The twenty-second Presidential election in American history took place on November 5th, 1872. It was the first election in which every state used a popular vote to determine its electors. Therefore, it felt like more of a...*democracy.*

For the most part, Ulysses Grant remained popular during his first term as President, especially with the majority of Republicans. He got his party's renomination. However, some Republicans did not like him so much. For one thing, they didn't like how Grant had a lot of friends in his Cabinet and ignored merit. A lot of his friends, as it would turn out, were a bit corrupt. As matter of fact, Vice President Schuyler Colfax was tied to the Crédit Mobilier of America scandal, in which many politicians were bribed for actions favorable to the railroad company Union Pacific. It would be just one of several scandals tied to the Grant administration. After Colfax was implicated, the Republican Party decided it might not be such a good idea to renominate him, so they instead nominated Henry Wilson, the U.S. Senator from Massachusetts, to be Grant's running mate.

Still, some Republicans, like Charles Sumner, weren't satisfied. Sumner was sick of the favoritism Grant showed to friends and family, calling it "Grantism." Some influential Republicans refused to support him, and actually started a new political party called the Liberal Republican Party. Those dang liberal Republicans.

They nominated Horace Greeley, a former U.S. Representative from New York and a well-known editor of the New York Tribune, for President. A journalist running for President? Crazy. They nominated Benjamin Gratz Brown, the Governor of Missouri, as his running mate.

Now here's something interesting. There was another fusion, or cross-endorsement, nomination this time. The Democratic Party *also* decided to nominate Horace Greeley for President and Benjamin Gratz Brown for Vice President. They even adopted the Liberal Republican platform, showing they were cool with Reconstruction policies. Really though, the main reason why they decided to go with the Liberal Republican nominees is because they wanted to take down Grant and knew by nominating different people it would just split his opposition.

How about some third parties? Well, there were at least three new ones. The Labor Reform Party tried to nominate a couple fellows, lawyer Charles O'Conor from New York, and Supreme Court justice David Davis from Illinois, but things just didn't work out. It was kind of doomed from the start.

Meanwhile, there was the Prohibition Party, which was formed to oppose the consumption and sale of alcohol. James Black, who founded the party and was a big temperance activist, was their first nominee for President. John Russell, another founder of the party, was his running mate.

By far the most interesting third party that ran for President in 1872, and maybe in American history, was the Equal Rights Party. The National Woman's Suffrage Association had supported a woman named Victoria Woodhull, an activist who publicly talked trash about the government only being made up of men. Despite the fact that women all across the country could not vote (except in sparsely populated Wyoming Territory and Utah Territory), Woodhull became the first woman to be nominated for President in American history. Frederick Douglass was nominated as her running mate, but he never acknowledged the nomination. Woodhull had little money and borrowed money from supporters for her campaign, usually not able to pay them back. Where are Super PACs when you need them, eh? So yeah, just let that sink in for a moment. In 1872, a woman ran for President with an African American as her running mate.

The two frontrunners, Grant and Greeley, were aggressively attacked. Grant for the corruption in his Cabinet, and Greeley for being an eccentric guy for his support of spiritualism (aka communicating with the dead), vegetarianism, prohibition, and socialism, all radical ideas at the time. Greeley had a rough campaign, and had the misfortune of a long history of positions published in his newspaper that opponents could nitpick. Even his own supporters were disappointed with him. On top of that, his wife died right before the election.

And here are the results...

Ulysses Grant easily won reelection, receiving 286 electoral votes and 55.6% of the popular vote. Horace Greeley received 43.8% of the popular vote, but, unfortunately he died three and a half weeks after election day. This was before the electors of the Electoral College had even met up yet. He would have received 66 electoral votes, but now those votes couldn't go to him, obviously, though three electors tried. Most of the remaining electoral votes then shifted to Thomas Hendricks, the former U.S. Senator from Indiana. All the other presidential candidates received less than 1% of the popular vote.

Henry Wilson became the eighteenth Vice President in American history.

This presidential election remains the only one in which a candidate died during the electoral process.

71.3% of the population voted in this election.

Turn the page for the next election, buddy.

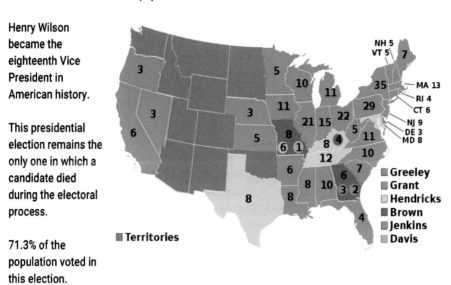

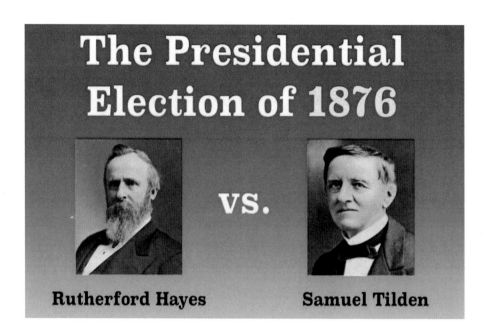

The Presidential Election of 1876

Rutherford Hayes vs. **Samuel Tilden**

The twenty-third Presidential election in American history took place on November 7th, 1876. Boy was this one controversial! President Ulysses Grant actually considered running for a third term, and he would have been the first to try, but he ultimately decided against it. This was probably a good idea since his administration continued to be accused of corruption and faced many scandals. Plus, the economy sucked. The country was in the middle of The Great Depression. Well, that's what they called it back then. After the real Great Depression happened in the 1930s, we now call this particular financial crisis the Panic of 1873.

So Grant was smart to decide against seeking a third term, but who would take his place? When the Republican National Convention assembled, several candidates were on the ballot. James Blaine, a U.S. Representative from Maine, looked to be the early favorite, but many Republicans argued Blaine couldn't win the general election due to scandals. Eventually they settled with Rutherford Hayes, the governor of Ohio. Rutherford was another Civil War hero, having fought with bravery and even getting wounded five times during the war. He was also known as a reformer. Plus, his beard was amazing. The Republicans chose William Wheeler, a U.S. Representative from New York, as his running mate.

The Democrats were feeling much better about their chances now that the economy was in ruins and Grant's friends had messed up the Republican image. They were fired up, and passionately supported Samuel Tilden, the governor of New York. Tilden was known as a new type of Democrat- a Bourbon Democrat. Bourbon Democrats were basically classical liberals who supported things like free trade and the gold standard and opposed things like imperialism.

The Democrats nominated Thomas Hendricks, the governor of Indiana, as Tilden's running mate.

So this election looked like a battle of governors. But wait, there's more!

A new political party, called the Greenback Party, had emerged to offer a third option. They wanted inflation through printing paper money, called greenbacks, and were quite anti-monopoly, bringing these both issues into the national spotlight. The Greenback Party nominated inventor and entrepreneur Peter Cooper for President. Cooper was an interesting fellow. Not only did *he* also have a terrific beard, he designed and built the first American steam locomotive. He was definitely not a politician, and was like 180 years old. Ok, he was actually just 85. Cooper was the oldest person ever nominated for President in American history.

Cooper's running mate was Samuel Fenton Cary, the former U.S. Representative from Ohio. As most third parties go, they stood little chance.

Meanwhile, it was shaping up to be a very close race between Hayes and Tilden. The two actually didn't campaign much, leaving that to their supporters. This election would mark the first one in which the new state of Colorado could participate. However, since it became a state in August, its state legislature, who happened to be Republican, chose the electors. In fact, this was the *last* election in which any state picked its electors this way. Keep this in mind when we look at the results here in a bit.

And here are the results...

Oh boy. We have a mess here. At first, it appeared as if Tilden was going to win. By midnight, he had 184 of the 185 electoral votes needed to win, and he led the popular vote by 250,000. Republicans called foul play, though, saying that in Southern states Democrats were using intimidation and bribery to get African Americans not to vote. Democrats also accused Republicans of not counting Tilden votes. But 20 electoral votes were disputed in four states-Florida, Louisiana, Oregon, and South Carolina.

In response, Congress immediately created an electoral commission to investigate and resolve the dispute.The commission had five U.S. Representatives, five U.S. Senators, and five Supreme Court justices. Five of the members of Congress were Democrat and five Republican. Of the five justices, two were Democrat and two Republican, and David Davis, the fifth justice–I mentioned him in the last episode actually–was an independent. However, Democrats in the Illinois legislature elected Davis to the U.S. Senate, in hopes that Davis would support Tilden. That plan backfired as David excused himself from the commission. Davis was replaced by Justice Joseph Bradley, hardly a political fellow, but still someone more aligned with the Republicans, and he would vote with them. Bradley's vote broke the tie along party lines, and in an 8 to 7 ruling, the commission decided to award the disputed electoral votes to Hayes. This made so many people angry that some even talked about a second civil war. To make the Democrats happy, the Republicans agreed to withdraw all remaining federal troops from the South, which officially ended Reconstruction. In other words, the North would no longer micro manage the South, and after this the South would attempt to go back to their pre-Civil War ways, especially with its discrimination against African Americans. This informal agreement became famously known as the Compromise of 1877.

So with 185 electoral votes, Rutherford Hayes won, becoming the nineteenth President in American history. William Wheeler became the nineteenth Vice President in American history.

Samuel J. Tilden finished with 184 electoral votes. Rutherford's victory was the smallest electoral vote victory in American history. To add insult to injury, Tilden won the popular vote by more than 250,000 votes. This is the only election in which a candidate for president received more than 50% of the popular vote but still didn't get

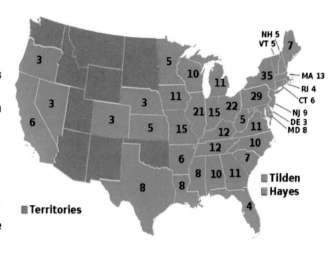

elected. Tilden said, "I can retire to public life with the consciousness that I shall receive from posterity the credit of having been elected to the highest position in the gift of the people, without any of the cares and responsibilities of the office." Understandably, people began to question the Electoral College after this election.

Peter Cooper had a solid showing for third place, finishing with about 1% of the popular vote.

This election was certainly unique. It was the first presidential election in 24 years in which a Democratic candidate won a majority of the popular vote. It was one of five elections in which the person who won the plurality, or most votes, did not win the election. The election of 1876 had the highest voter turnout in American history. It was the last one to occur prior to the end of Reconstruction, and it'd be another twenty years before a Southern state would again vote for a Republican presidential hopeful.

81.8% of the population voted in this election.

Turn the page for the next election, buddy.

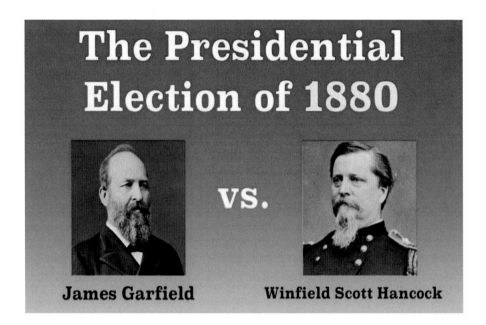

The Presidential Election of 1880

VS.

James Garfield   **Winfield Scott Hancock**

The twenty-fourth Presidential election in American history took place on November 2, 1880.

Back in 1876, while running for President, Rutherford Hayes promised he would not seek a second term. Rutherford actually stayed true to his word. In 1880, he was leaving that job open for someone else. But who else? Well, Republicans had a hard time figuring out who would take his place. Republican leaders met in June in what would become the longest Republican National Convention in history. Two major factions within the Republican Party made the decision for a nominee a difficult one. One faction, the Stalwarts, tended to revolve around the U.S. Senator from New York named Roscoe Conkling. They generally favored a thing called patronage (also known as the spoils system) which basically said you should reward the people who got you elected. The other faction, the Half-Breeds (they got that name because their opponents called them only "half Republican"), revolved around the U.S. Senator from Maine named James Blaine. Yep, Blaine from Maine. The Half-Breeds generally did not like patronage, saying people should be appointed on merit alone and not by political favors or obligations.

That was pretty much the only big issue dividing the Republicans, surprisingly. After deciding against it in 1876, Ulysses Grant shocked several people when he decided to run for a third term. Many Republicans were all for it, but he had opponents. The aforementioned James Blaine, John Sherman, the brother of Civil War general William Tecumseh Sherman and former U.S. Senator from Ohio, and James Garfield, a U.S. Representative from Ohio. It took a long time, but the Republicans ultimately nominated neither a Stalwart nor a Half-Breed. They nominated a guy who definitely did not expect to get nominated- James Garfield. Some of the

Stalwarts weren't so sure about Garfield, so Chester Arthur, a Stalwart and Chairman of the New York Republican Party, was nominated as his running mate.

Under the shadow of Samuel Tilden's devastating defeat four years earlier, the Democrats held their convention soon after. The two leading candidates were Major General Winfield Scott Hancock of Pennsylvania and Thomas Bayard, a U.S. Senator from Delaware. The Democrats finally had their war hero- Hancock served most of his life in the Army. He was a Civil War veteran, and the dude even fought in the Mexican American War, for crying out loud. So yeah, Bayard didn't stand a chance. Hancock was the nominee, with William Hayden English, a businessman and former U.S. Representative from Indiana, as his running mate.

The Greenback Party had gained some momentum since their first presidential try in 1876. Hoping to actually win some actual electoral votes this time, they nominated James Weaver, a U.S. Representative and Civil War general from Iowa. Unlike Garfield and Hancock, he went around the country giving speeches to promote his campaign. Weaver's running mate was Barzillai Chambers, a surveyor and lawyer who fought with the Confederates in the Civil War, believe it or not.

What was fascinating to me about this election is that the Presidential candidates didn't seem to disagree a whole lot, although you wouldn't know it living at the time. For example, a hot button issue in the final weeks before election day was Chinese immigration. In reality, the Republicans, Democrats, and Greenbackers all wanted to limit Chinese immigration. They all agreed! So what's the issue?

And here are the results...

Boy was this one a squeaker. It was extremely close with the popular vote, but in the Electoral College not so much. James Garfield won, becoming the twentieth President in American history. He received 214 electoral votes.

Winfield Hancock received 155 electoral votes, but that may be deceiving. Fewer than 2,000 votes separated Hancock and Garfield, making this election the smallest popular vote victory ever recorded.

Looking at the electoral map, do you notice a pattern?

Yep, Hancock dominated the South, and Garfield the North.

James Weaver finished third, not getting any electoral votes but finishing with a solid 3% of the popular vote.

Chester Arthur became the twentieth Vice President in American history.

James Garfield was in office only 200 days. Two and a half months of that he was in a bed dying. On July 2nd, 1881, he was shot by a literally insane dude who was upset that Garfield didn't give him a job. Garfield was the second President assassinated in American history.

78% of the population voted in this election.

Turn the page for the next election, buddy.

The Presidential Election of 1884

vs.

Grover Cleveland   **James Blaine**

The twenty-fifth Presidential election in American history took place on November 4, 1884. Chester Arthur had become President after the assassination of James Garfield. His health had been declining, and he honestly didn't know if he would make it another term if he ran for reelection. Still, a lot of people wanted him to run, so he gave it a try. James Blaine, the former Speaker of the House and U.S. Senator from Maine, was the favorite for the Republican nomination, but George Edmunds, a U.S. Senator from Vermont, also had a good chance to win it. Two notable people that many wanted to run were Civil War general William Tecumseh Sherman and Abraham Lincoln's son, Robert Todd Lincoln, who at this time was the Secretary of War. Both Sherman and Lincoln strongly *did not* want to run for President, no matter how much people tried to talk them into it.

Ultimately, the Republicans went with a name that many already recognized throughout the country- James Blaine. After nominating Blaine, they went with John Logan, a U.S. Senator from Illinois, as his running mate.

The Democratic Party chose Grover Cleveland, the Governor of New York, who was known as a man of integrity who spent much of his career fighting political corruption, so I don't know why the heck they nominated him. The Democratic Party went with a familiar face for Cleveland's running mate. Thomas Hendricks, the former Governor of Indiana, who ran for Vice President on the ticket with Samuel Tilden back in 1876. Remember that one? Hendricks won. Oops, he actually lost that one, but was back for another try, this time with a *different* classical liberal.

There were several third parties. The Greenback Party was back for a third try, hoping to gain even more momentum. They nominated Benjamin Butler, the former Governor of

Massachusetts, with Absolom West, a plantation owner and former Confederate general from Mississippi, as his running mate.

Another political party that was continuing to pick up momentum and continuing to hate alcohol was the Prohibition Party. This time they nominated John St. John (that's his actual name), a former governor of Kansas, with William Daniel as his running mate, a lawyer and local politician from Maryland.

The second notable woman to run for President, Belva Ann Lockwood, ran with the Equal Rights Party. The former teacher and principal was the first female to actually appear on official ballots, so that's pretty cool. Yep, she still didn't stand a chance. Activist Marietta Stow was her running mate.

The two top candidates were personally attacked leading up to the election. Blaine, for being accused of using his influence for special favors, and Cleveland, for fathering an illegitimate child.

And here are the results...

Grover Cleveland won, becoming the twenty-second President in American history. He received 219 electoral votes, and James Blaine received 182 electoral votes, but this is a little deceiving, as the election was actually a lot closer. In fact, if it weren't for the fact that Cleveland barely won his home state of New York by just over 1,000 votes, he would have lost the election. New York had 36 electoral votes up for grabs, and thanks to our lovely Electoral College, Cleveland got all of them. It was a narrow popular vote overall, with Cleveland winning 48.9% and Blaine winning 48.3%. John St. John and his magnificent mustache finished third with 1.5% of the popular vote, and Benjamin Butler finished fourth with 1.3% of the popular vote. All other nominees got less than 1%.

Thomas Hendricks became the twenty-first Vice President in American history.

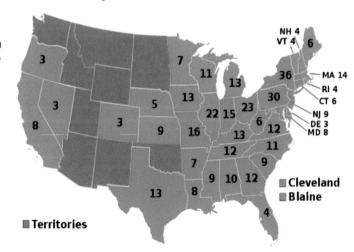

Cleveland's victory broke the longest losing streak for any major political party in American history, which was six consecutive elections. This might be a spoiler alert, but Grover Cleveland was the only Democratic President elected between 1861 and 1913.

77.5% of the population voted in this election.

Turn the page for the next election, buddy.

The Presidential Election of 1888

vs.

Grover Cleveland   **Benjamin Harrison**

The twenty-sixth Presidential election in American history took place on November 6, 1888, exactly 93 years before I was born. Grover Cleveland had a solid first term. The country was at peace and the economy was fantastic. He even got married to Frances Folsom, who, at 21 years old, became the youngest First Lady in American history. Cleveland was a fairly popular dude with lots of integrity. Now, if Cleveland was alive today, he'd be called a libertarian, and many Americans weren't quite on board with that. He vetoed a lot of bills, tried to reduce government spending, had a non interventionist foreign policy, and wanted free trade.

Cleveland was unanimously renominated by the Democratic Party, which was special because this was the first time a Democratic President had been renominated since Martin Van Buren in 1840. Since his former Vice President, Thomas Hendricks, had died while in office, he needed a new one, so the Democrats nominated Allen Thurman, a former U.S. Senator from Ohio, to run with him this time.

You know how I mentioned free trade? Well many people were upset with Cleveland's free trade leanings, and they wanted a higher tariff to protect American industries. Many Americans in industrial states wanted to vote against Cleveland because they feared losing their jobs, and they looked again to the Republicans.

James Blaine decided not to run for President this time because he feared he might just further divide the Republican Party. He backed both Benjamin Harrison, a U.S. Senator from Indiana and grandson of former President William Henry Harrison, and John Sherman, who was still a U.S. Senator from Ohio and now running a second time.

The Republicans went with Harrison, mostly because he was a Civil War veteran who was popular with other veterans. He also could give a darn good speech. Oh yeah, and he lived in a swing state. Thanks Electoral College! Levi Morton, a New York City banker and former U.S. Representative and Minister to France, was his running mate.

It's time for third parties! I will only mention two of them as the others were pretty irrelevant. No offense, United Labor Party!

The Prohibition Party kept gaining momentum. They nominated Clinton Fisk, a general from New York, with John Brooks, a religious scholar and pastor from Kentucky, as his running mate.

Members of a new political party, the Union Labor Party, were a ragtag bunch with wide ranging views, but they were all united to fight for worker rights. They nominated Alson Streeter, a former Greenbacker, farmer, and miner from Illinois. His running mate was a lumberman named Charles Cunningham, from Arkansas.

The campaigns between the two front runners, Cleveland and Harrison, were intense, as it looked to be a super close election. The main issue, of course, was tariffs. Cleveland wanted less, and Harrison more. While Cleveland still did not actively campaign as most presidential candidates did not before him, Harrison did, enthusiastically giving many speeches from his front porch of his Indianapolis home to many newspaper reporters. His front porch campaign was similar to James Garfield, and it worked well for him, so why not?

So here is one development that was pretty messed up. Leading up to the election, it was exposed that William Wade Dudley, the Treasurer of the Republican National Committee, was caught buying votes in Indiana for Harrison. Remember, Indiana was a swing state so this was a big deal. The outcry of this scandal is a big reason why ballots after this were cast in secret and not out in the open.

And here are the results...

Benjamin Harrison won, becoming the twenty-third President in American history. Now, this goes beyond the shadiness going down in Indiana, as Harrison probably would have won anyway. Cleveland couldn't even win the electoral vote in his home state this time.

Back in 1884 he was lucky to win New York and it gave him the election. This time, if he would have won New York he would have been reelected as well. I guess what goes around comes around, Grover.

Harrison received 233 electoral votes, and Cleveland won 168 electoral votes. Cleveland did receive more votes overall, though. He won 48.6% of the popular vote, compared to Harrison winning 47.8%. This was the third of five American presidential elections in which the winner of the election didn't win the popular vote. Clinton Fisk finished third in the popular vote, with 2.2%, and Alson Streeter finished fourth with 1.3% of the popular vote.

Levi Morton became the twenty-second Vice President in American history.

As you can see on this lovely map, Harrison dominated in the North and out West, and Cleveland dominated in the South.

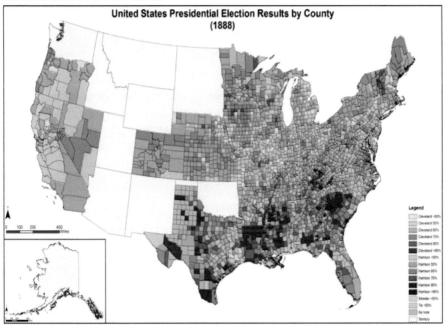

As First Lady Frances Folsom, now Frances Cleveland, left the White House at the end of Grover's term, she is reported to have told the White House staff to take good care of the building as they would be returning in four years. Was she right? Did she actually predict the future? Find out in the next chapter, eh?

79.3% of the population voted in this election.

Turn the page for the next election, buddy.

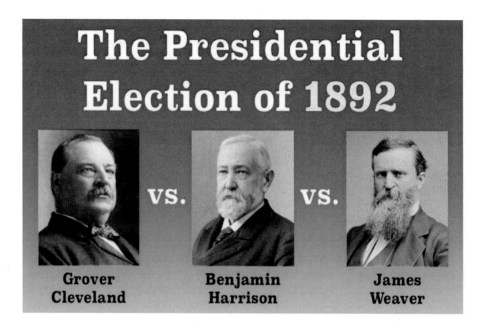

The Presidential Election of 1892

Grover Cleveland   VS.   Benjamin Harrison   VS.   James Weaver

The twenty-seventh Presidential election in American history took place on November 8, 1892. Benjamin Harrison had a rough term as President, and even though he had doubts himself, he decided to run for reelection. The Republican Party went ahead and renominated him, despite potential challenges from former candidates John Sherman, the U.S. Senator from Ohio, and James Blaine, who was now the U.S. Secretary of State.

Levi Morton would not be renominated, however. Back in 1890, Harrison supported the Lodge Bill, an election law meant to help the black vote in the South as a way to fight Jim Crow laws, but it didn't pass. Harrison blamed Morton for the bill's failure, and at the Republican convention, Morton was replaced by Whitelaw Reid, the editor of the New York Tribune and recent U.S. Ambassador to France.

Guess who's back? Grover's back!
After winning the popular vote but losing the electoral vote in 1888, Grover Cleveland was back with a vengeance in 1892. While many were ready for a return to his policies, he did face opponents like David Hill, the U.S. Senator and former governor of New York. However, Cleveland survived to become the first Democrat nominated a third time to run for President. The Democrats nominated Adlai Stevenson, a former U.S. Representative from Illinois, for Vice President. Stevenson was an interesting choice because he favored greenbacks and free silver to inflate the currency while Cleveland was a gold standard guy who didn't like just printing money. Cleveland was cool with Stevenson on the ticket, though, as it provided some balance.

Still, a lot of Americans were not satisfied with the two-party system, and by this time a new movement had emerged. The previous year, alliances made up of poor cotton farmers in the

South, wheat farmers in the Plains states, labor unions in the North, and Republicans in South, all joined forces to create a new political party. They called it the People's Party. More commonly known as the Populists, they generally were hostile to banks, railroad corporations, the gold standard, and even city folk. Basically, they were united against the so-called "elites." The Populists had their first convention in Omaha, Nebraska, which was a Populist hot spot. They nominated James Weaver, the former U.S. Representative from Iowa, who had previously ran for President in the Greenback Party back in 1880 but lost. His running mate was James Field, the Attorney General of Virginia.

The Prohibition Party was still going strong. At their convention, there were talks of merging with the Populists, but it just never panned out. They nominated John Bidwell, one of the original pioneers to head out west and a former U.S. Representative from California. Texas religious leader James Cranfill, also known as The Reverend J.B. Cranfill, was Bidwell's running mate.

One interesting political party that emerged in 1892 was the Socialist Labor Party. They were only on the ballot in five states, but had a unique platform that called for getting rid of the positions of President and Vice President. So they nominated camera inventor Simon Wing for President and socialist activist Charles Matchett for Vice President, even though both would willingly give up their positions after getting elected. Weird.

Just like the last presidential election, debate over tariffs dominated the campaigns. Harrison defended his support of the McKinley Tariff, while Cleveland continued to argue for tariff reductions. The campaigns all stopped after Harrison's wife, First Lady Caroline Harrison, passed away in October from tuberculosis.

And here are the results...

Grover Cleveland won, becoming the twenty-fourth President in American history. He received 277 electoral votes. He also won 46% of the popular vote, which was actually his worst showing yet, but a win is a win. Benjamin Harrison received 145 electoral votes, and 43% of the popular vote. Populist James Weaver finished third, with 22 electoral votes and 8.5% of the popular vote. He became the only third party candidate between 1860 and 1912 to win electoral votes. He did especially well in the West and South.

John Bidwell received 2.2% of the popular vote, the best performance by the Prohibition Party yet. All other candidates received less than 1%.

Adlai Stevenson became the twenty-third Vice President in American history.

This was the first time incumbent presidents were defeated in two consecutive elections. This wouldn't happen again until 1980.

Up to that point in history, Cleveland was one of only two people, the other being Andrew Jackson, to win the popular vote in three American presidential elections. He, of course, is the only President in American history to serve two non-consecutive terms in office.

74.7% of the population voted in this election.

Turn the page for the next election, buddy.

■ Territories

NH 4
VT 4

MA 15
RI 4
CT 6
NJ 10
DE 3
MD 8

■ Cleveland
■ Harrison
■ Weaver

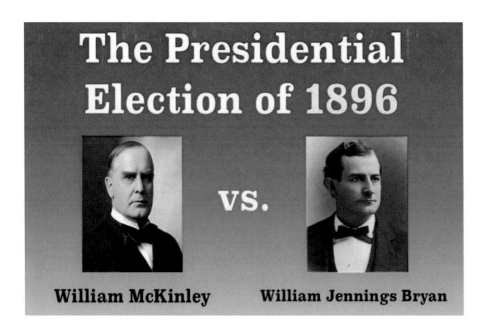

The Presidential Election of 1896

William McKinley   William Jennings Bryan

The twenty-eighth Presidential election in American history took place on November 3, 1896. Turnout was high, and people were saying things like "this is the most important election ever." Yeah right, as if they don't say that *every* election.

Grover Cleveland's second term didn't go so well. For most of it, the country had been stuck in a severe economic depression. And while the Populist Movement was at its peak, with poor people pointing fingers at "the man," everybody seemed to be losing money during this time, even the rich.

The Republicans rallied behind a new face on the national scene- William McKinley, the former governor of Ohio. They nominated Garret Hobart as his running mate, a former New Jersey legislator.

The Democratic Party had generally shifted away from Cleveland to a more "free silver" monetary policy, calling for inflation to help ease the economic crisis. In fact, they had adopted several of the Populist ideas. At first, there was no obvious successor to Cleveland, and several candidates emerged, like ol' "Sliver Dick" himself, Richard P. Bland, the former U.S. Representative from Missouri. However, soon another dude stood out quite a bit, mostly for his incredibly awesome speeches. That dude was William Jennings Bryan.

Bryan, a former U.S. Representative and lawyer from Nebraska, gave his famous "Cross of Gold" speech at the Democratic National Convention. In the speech, he sounded very much like a Populist, passionately attacking big-city corporations and the gold standard, while calling for government relief for farmers and others hurt by the depression. His speech was so dramatic that after he was done some delegates carried him on their shoulders as if he was the quarterback who had just scored the winning touchdown. Needless to say, Bryan got the nomination.The Democrats nominated Arthur Sewall, a shipbuilder from Maine, to be his running mate.

The Populist Party also endorsed Willing Jennings Bryan, since his party basically co-opted their ideas, and so did the newly formed Silver Party, so it was quite a fusionist election. Bryan is still the youngest person ever nominated by a major political party for president. He was 36 on election day.

Meanwhile, Democrats who were not on board with the Free Silver movement formed their own political party called the National Democratic Party. Also known as Gold Democrats, they were more aligned with Cleveland and would absolutely not support Bryan. They met in August and nominated John Palmer, a U.S. Senator from Illinois, for President, and Simon Buckner, the former Governor of Kentucky, for Vice President. Palmer was 79 years old and Buckner 73, making the two the oldest combined presidential ticket in American history.

The Prohibition Party split in two for this election. Some wanted to go beyond just the Prohibition issue, and so they went off and formed a different Prohibition Party. So basically, the Prohibition Party had two tickets- Joshua Levering and Hale Johnson forming the traditional single issue ticket, and Charles Bentley and James Southgate forming the more broad-based issues ticket.

However, let's get real here. McKinley and Bryan were the only ones who stood a chance. And so, this became a battle of the Williams. Unlike any presidential candidate before him, Bryan criss-crossed the country to campaign. He traveled 18,000 miles in 3 months. In just 100 days, he gave over 500 speeches. On one of those days, while he was in St. Louis, he gave 36 speeches in one day. By doing this, he reached millions of people, and everywhere he went huge crowds showed up. He didn't get much sleep, and often lost his voice, explaining in a hoarse voice he left his real voice at the previous places he visited to keep firing up the people.

Meanwhile, William McKinley mostly just stayed home. He didn't have to criss-cross the country, as his buddy Mark Hanna did all the work and brought the people to McKinley's front porch. Hanna orchestrated a masterful campaign that was successful at raising millions of dollars, much more than Bryan could raise. In fact, Hanna literally invented a new form of campaign financing that has been the norm ever since. He went straight to businesses to get donations, making propositions. The McKinley campaign was successful at making many businesses fear a Bryan presidency.

And here are the results...

William McKinley won, becoming the twenty-fifth President in American history. He received 271 electoral votes and 51% of the popular vote. He did particularly well in the East and Northeast. William Jennings Bryan received 176 electoral votes, and 46.7% of the popular vote. He particularly did well with farmers in the South, West, and Midwest. I guess that's no surprise.

John Palmer finished third, with just under 1% of the popular vote. Joshua Levering finished fourth, just over 3,000 votes behind Palmer.

Garret Hobart became the twenty-fourth Vice President in American history.

While Bryan's defeat
was a blow to Populist momentum, many of the ideas brought into the mainstream during his campaign would stick around long after this election.

79.3% of the population voted in this election.

Turn the page for the next election, buddy.

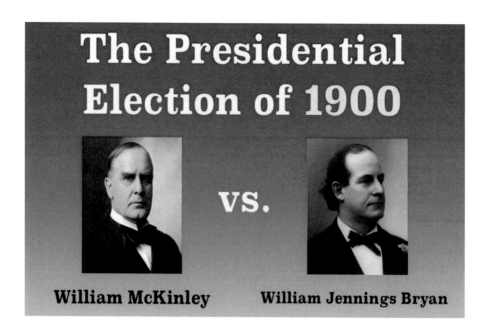

The Presidential Election of 1900

William McKinley   vs.   **William Jennings Bryan**

The twenty-ninth Presidential election in American history took place on November 6, 1900, exactly 81 years before my birthday. Oh boy, we got ourselves another rematch!

During William McKinley's first term, the United States, according to many indicators, became much stronger. The economy was back to being awesome, and the country had joined the "Imperial Club." That's right, America was now officially an imperialist country, thanks to becoming involved in the Spanish-American War. The United States easily defeated Spain, gaining the colonies of Puerto Rico, Guam, the Philippines, and even Cuba for a little while. Sure, there were some shady sides to this war and its aftermath, like the Philippine-American War, which raged on. However, Americans were feeling pretty darn good about themselves overall.

The war represented American entry into world affairs, actually acting out what the Monroe Doctrine promised 75 years prior. Since then, the United States has had a pretty consistent role in policing various conflicts all over the world.

Anyway, so McKinley was popular and easily renominated. However, his Vice President, Garret Hobart, had passed away while in office, and McKinley needed a replacement to run with him. One name floating around was New York governor Theodore Roosevelt. He was the former Assistant Secretary of the Navy under McKinley, and a somewhat reckless "war hero" of the Spanish American War. Thomas C. Platt, the New York State Republican Party boss, strongly disliked Roosevelt and wanted him out of the state, so he pressured McKinley to agree to let him be his running mate. Although Roosevelt wasn't too excited about the possibility of becoming Vice President, he accepted the nomination anyway.

Early on, the Democrats were leaning toward nominating another Spanish American War hero, George Dewey, who was the Admiral of the Navy and from Vermont. Dewey made a fool out of himself, however, so that ultimately opened the door again to William Jennings Bryan, who still had a large force of passionate supporters. Interestingly, they chose former Vice President Adlai Stevenson as his running mate. Stevenson was the first former Vice President to win renomination for that position with a different presidential candidate.

So it was another battle of the Williams! However, let's not forget third party candidates. By this time, the Populist Party, or People's Party, had splintered. The faction known as the "Fusion" Populists again supported William Jennings Bryan for the nomination. But the "Middle of the Road" Populists nominated Wharton Barker, a publicist and investor from Pennsylvania, with Ignatius Donnelly, a former U.S. Representative from Minnesota and amateur scientist, as his running mate.

The Prohibition Party reunited and was excited for this election. They nominated John Woolley, a lawyer, reformed alcoholic, and public speaker originally from Ohio. Henry Metcalf, a businessman from Boston, was Woolley's running mate.

There were several other third parties, but the only one I will mention here is the Social Democratic Party, a new political party that began after a large group of people left the Socialist Labor Party. At their first convention in Indianapolis, they nominated Indiana native Eugene Debs as their candidate, who was famously known as a national union leader and one of the founding members of the Industrial Workers of the World. Get used to hearing the name "Eugene Debs" in future elections. The Social Democratic party nominated Job Harriman, a minister also from Indiana, as Debs' running mate.

Again, it was a battle of the Williams, and this election was quite similar to the 1896 election, except this time the economy was in MUCH better shape, so Bryan's call for Free Silver did not gain as much traction. Also, this time around Bryan vocally attacked McKinley's imperialist foreign policy. While Bryan had supported the original war, he was against the continual occupation of the Philippines, saying McKinley had just replaced a bad Spanish tyranny with a bad American one.

Just like last time, Bryan traveled across the country giving many, many speeches, but Theodore Roosevelt also did the same. Roosevelt was also young like Bryan, and had a lot of the same energy. He would end up being an important force to reckon with in this election.

And here are the results...

William McKinley won reelection, receiving 292 electoral votes. William Jennings Bryan finished as runner up again, this time receiving 155 electoral votes. McKinley won 51.6% of the popular vote, better than in his first election, while Bryan had a worse showing this time finishing with 45.5% of the popular vote.

John Woolley finished third, with 1.5% of the popular vote. All other candidates finished with less than 1% of the popular vote.

Theodore Roosevelt became the twenty-fifth Vice President in American history, and while he wasn't the most excited for that position, I have a feeling he will be getting a promotion soon.

73.2% of the population voted in this election.

Turn the page for the next election, buddy.

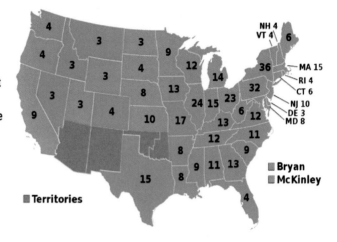

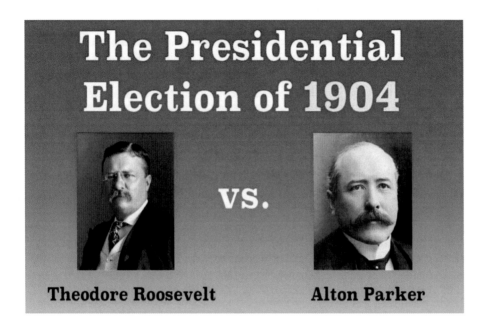

The Presidential Election of 1904

vs.

Theodore Roosevelt   **Alton Parker**

The thirtieth Presidential election in American history took place on November 8, 1904. Theodore Roosevelt was running for reelection. Hold up, Teddy Roosevelt? He was running for reelection? What happened to McKinley? Well, let's rewind three years.

Back on September 6, 1901, President William McKinley was shot twice as he was shaking hands at the Temple of Music in Buffalo, New York. McKinley's wounds became infected, and he died eight days later. It was after this that the Secret Service provided full-time presidential protection, by the way.

Vice President Theodore Roosevelt was sworn in and became the twenty-sixth President in American history. At age 42, he was the youngest man to ever become President. But he wasn't intimidated. He went straight to work, promising the "average Joe" fairness, fighting the giant corporations that had monopolies on various markets, championing the construction of the Panama Canal, and regulating the railroads, food and drugs. He made conservation a top priority, establishing a bunch of national parks, forests, and monuments. Later on, he would even help end the Russo-Japanese War, becoming the first President (and American, for that matter) to earn a Nobel Peace Prize for doing so. More than any President before him, he welcomed the press with open arms. After noticing reporters just outside the White House getting wet in the rain one day, he let them in and gave them their own room. By doing so, he basically invented the presidential press briefing.

He truly became a man of the people, and because of this, he was extremely popular. Some fellow Republicans, however, called him a radical due to his Progressive policies, and they tried to get Mark Hanna to run against him as the official nominee. However, Hanna died in

February, and no serious contender rose to compete with Roosevelt. So Roosevelt was the nominee, but to make the conservatives happy the Republicans nominated Charles Fairbanks, the likable U.S. Senator from Indiana, as his running mate.

The Democrats had a hard time finding a strong nominee that could compete with Roosevelt. William Jennings Bryan didn't want to run a third time, and they even asked Grover Cleveland to run again, but he turned it down, too. A lot of Bryan's supporters flocked to the New York newspaper publisher turned- U.S. Representative William Randolph Hearst. But Hearst frankly scared many Democrats to death, so many of them turned to Alton Parker, the Chief Judge of the New York Court of Appeals. They nominated Henry Davis, a former U.S. Senator from West Virginia, as his running mate. At 80 years old, Davis was the oldest major-party candidate ever to be nominated for national office.

I will mention two third parties for this election. A new political party called the Socialist Party of America, or just Socialist Party for short, nominated a well-known socialist–perhaps one of the original socialists–Eugene Debs. Debs ran and lost in 1900, but his support seemed to be growing. The Socialist Party nominated Ben Hanford, a printer based out of New York.

The Prohibition Party nominated Silas Swallow, a Methodist preacher from Pennsylvania with an awkward name, for President with George Washington Carroll, a Texas oilman and lumberman with a more familiar name, as his running mate.

The campaigning in 1904 was fairly low-key. Maybe it was because most everyone knew Alton Parker didn't stand a chance against the popular Roosevelt. While Roosevelt was charismatic and energetic, Parker was boring and didn't get even Democrats excited. Plus, Parker and Roosevelt agreed on most issues, so this election became more about the difference between their personalities.

And here are the results...

Theodore Roosevelt easily won reelection. In fact, it was a landslide. Roosevelt received 336 electoral votes and Alton Parker only received 140 electoral votes. Roosevelt absolutely dominated everywhere except the South. Roosevelt became the first Republican to win the state of Missouri since 1868. The popular vote was just as lopsided, with Roosevelt getting 56.4% and Parker getting just 37.6%.

Eugene Debs came in third, not winning electoral votes but getting a respectable 3% of the popular vote. Silas Swallow came in fourth, getting 1.9% of the popular vote.

Charles Fairbanks became the twenty-sixth Vice President in American history.

Teddy Roosevelt became the first President to win an election...after becoming President not by election...in American history.

65.2% of the population voted in this election.

Turn the page for the next election, buddy.

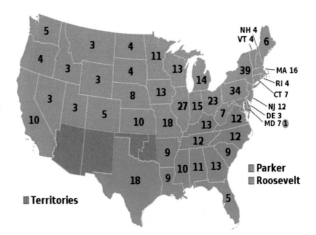

■ Territories

■ Parker
■ Roosevelt

NH 4
VT 4
6
MA 16
RI 4
CT 7
NJ 12
DE 3
MD 7 ①

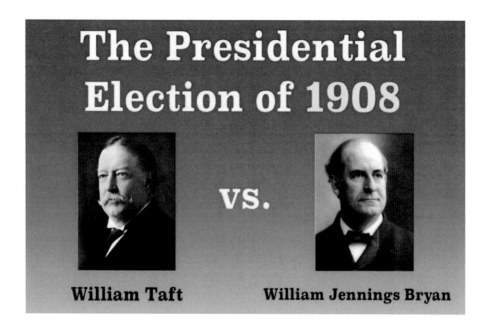

The Presidential Election of 1908

VS.

William Taft

William Jennings Bryan

The thirty-first Presidential election in American history took place on November 3, 1908. Throughout his presidency, Theodore Roosevelt had managed to gain fans from both the Republican and Democratic parties. His ideas were what we now call "progressive," but by 1908 everybody seemed to want to be called "progressive."

While Roosevelt didn't get as much accomplished in his second term, he remained very popular. After the last election, he promised he would not run for a third term, and instead fully endorsed his close friend and the Secretary of War, William Howard Taft, to continue the progressive reforms that he had started. Even though Taft had much rather be on the Supreme Court than be President, he couldn't turn Roosevelt down.

The Republican nomination process marked the first time a presidential preference primary happened, where delegates were chosen from multiple states. At the convention, most Republicans would do whatever Roosevelt recommended, and Taft was officially nominated. Although, Roosevelt seemed to get more cheers than he did. A lot of them really wanted Roosevelt to run again, after all. They nominated James Sherman, a U.S. Representative from New York, as Taft's running mate.

Perhaps the main reason why William Jennings Bryan did not run for President in 1904 is because he agreed with Roosevelt on many issues. In fact, perhaps Roosevelt stole some of his ideas. Now that Roosevelt was out of the picture, Bryan actually argued he was the more logical successor to Roosevelt than Taft. Despite the fact that Bryan had lost the previous two times he ran, he remained very popular, and the Democratic Party went with him again. Third time's a charm, right? The Democrats nominated John Kern, a former member of the Indiana Senate, as Bryan's running mate.

While there were at least five third parties who tried for nationwide campaigns, the two biggest were the Socialist Party and the Prohibition Party, just like in 1904.

The Socialist Party nominated Eugene Debs again for President. Like Bryan, he had also lost twice before. Third time's a charm, right? Just like in 1904, Ben Hanford, the printer based out of New York, was Debs' running mate.

The Prohibition Party nominated Eugene Chafin, a lawyer originally from Wisconsin, for President, with Aaron Watkins, an education administrator, lawyer, and minister from Ohio, as his running mate.

This was yet another battle of the Williams. William Jennings Bryan ran another intense campaign filled with much traveling and speeches, but the Free Silver movement was no longer strong, so this time he spoke out against the special interests in Washington. His slogan was "Shall the People Rule?"

However, like Roosevelt, William Howard Taft's platform had many of the same solutions as Bryan.Taft's campaign used the slogan "Vote for Taft now, you can vote for Bryan anytime." sarcastically referring to Bryan's two past failed campaigns. That's shady!

This would be the first presidential election in which Oklahoma could participate, as it was now a state.

And here are the results...

William Howard Taft won, becoming the twenty-seventh President in American history. Taft won pretty handily. He received 321 electoral votes and 51.6% of the popular vote.

William Jennings Bryan finished second place yet again. It was his worst defeat yet, and he wouldn't run for President again after this. He received 162 electoral votes and 43% of the popular vote.

Looking at this map, you can see that Taft did well mostly in the North and out West, but Bryan did well in the South and better in new random regions all over the country.

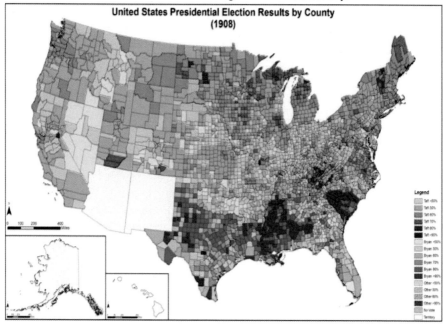

Bryan's support was more diverse than ever, yet still too short.

Eugene Debs came in third again, with 2.8% of the popular vote. Eugene Chafin finished fourth, with 1.7% of the popular vote.

James Sherman became the twenty-seventh Vice President in American history.

Indeed, it was Taft to continue the legacy of Teddy Roosevelt, not Bryan. But would Teddy approve of how his good friend did as President? Find out in the next episode!

65.4% of the population voted in this election.

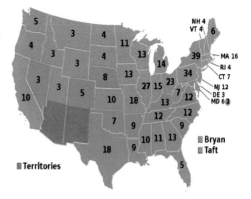

Turn the page for the next election, buddy.

The Presidential Election of 1912

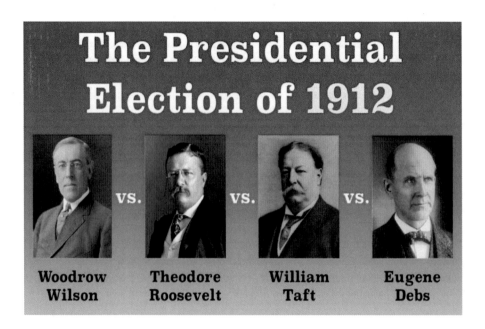

Woodrow Wilson vs. Theodore Roosevelt vs. William Taft vs. Eugene Debs

The thirty-second Presidential election in American history took place on November 5, 1912. Oh yeah! This was the election that was completely and utterly messed up. It was weird, man. It was really weird.

How weird? Well look at the electoral map, for crying out loud.

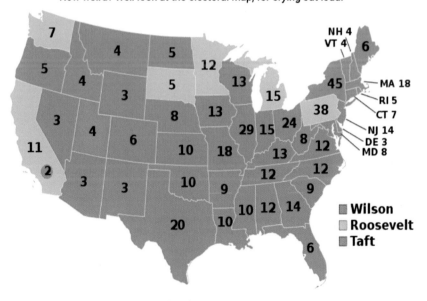

What the heck is that?

However, I'm ahead of myself. Let's go back a bit. The Taft presidency was supposed to be Theodore Roosevelt 2.0. But right off the bat, it just wasn't that way. Taft was, like, *his own person.* He fired Cabinet members that Roosevelt had approved of or appointed. While Taft continued to fight trusts, he placed less of a commitment to conservation, labor unions, and restrictions on the employment of women and children. Soon there was a clear split in the Republican Party, between the more conservative-leaning Republicans led by Taft, and the Progressive Republicans, led by Teddy Roosevelt.

After traveling around the world with his family for more than a year, Roosevelt came home to one of the biggest receptions ever given in New York City. Initially neutral about giving his opinion about how his friend was doing as President, that changed when eventually a bunch of Progressive Republicans had convinced Roosevelt to run against Taft in 1912.

The Republicans expanded their primaries to include even more delegates from across the country to the national convention to choose their nominee. Going into the convention, Roosevelt actually had more delegates than Taft did. Taft's people, however, controlled the convention and essentially shut out many of the Roosevelt delegates. This, of course, made Roosevelt very angry, and he and his supporters stormed out of the convention. Not since the election of 1872 had there been such a major divide within the Republican Party.

In fact, Roosevelt and his supporters completely abandoned the Republicans, two weeks later meeting up to create their own political party, called the Progressive Party. These Progressives nominated Roosevelt for President (well duh) and Hiram Johnson, the Governor of California, as his running mate. At the convention, Roosevelt passionately called for what he called a "New Nationalism." Their platform sought a minimum wage for women, an 8-hour workday, a child labor law, a social security system, a national health service, and the direct election of U.S. senators, among other things. Afterward, Roosevelt told reporters he felt as strong as a bull moose. After that, the Progressive Party became popularly known as the "Bull Moose Party."

Despite the excitement of the Bull Moose Party, the Republicans pressed on with Taft as their candidate and Vice President James Sherman again as his running mate. Believe it or not, Sherman was the first incumbent Vice President to be nominated for reelection since John Calhoun way back in 1828.

Meanwhile, the Democratic Party, who hadn't done so well in presidential elections since, I don't know, *before the Civil War,* saw this major split of the Republican Party as a golden opportunity. They had a bit of drama as well at their own convention. Originally it looked like Champ Clark, the Speaker of the House from Missouri, was going to be the guy, but he failed to get the two-thirds majority needed to secure the nomination. In second place was Woodrow Wilson, the Governor of New Jersey. Wilson didn't really think he had a chance, but then William Jennings Bryan decided to endorse him, and Bryan still had a lot of fans, so therefore had a lot of influence. On the 46th ballot...that's right, I said *46th*, the Democrats nominated Wilson, with Thomas Marshall, the Governor of Indiana, as his running mate.

So that's it? Oh heck no it's not.

In 1912, Eugene Debs ran for President a fourth time, trying to keep together a Socialist Party that was also splintering. Debs was by this time a recognizable name across the nation, and his running mate was Emil Seidel, the former mayor of Milwaukee. Seidel was the first ever Socialist mayor of an American city, as matter of fact.

The Prohibition Party responded to Eugene running again by having their Eugene run again. Eugene Chafin gave it a second try with Aaron Watkins again as his running mate.

The campaigns were dominated by the rivalry between Taft and Roosevelt, former friends who now seemed like bitter enemies. With those two fighting, the election looked to be a lock for Wilson, which was lucky for the Democrats because Wilson wasn't the most charismatic person.

Teddy Roosevelt was charismatic, but critics said he was running more for his ego and for spoiling the election for the Republicans than for actually reforming the country. Roosevelt campaigned like crazy, traveling around 10,000 miles and visiting 34 states. While he was in Milwaukee, an unemployed saloonkeeper named John Schrank shot him right before he was about to give a speech. As it turns out, the bullet did not penetrate his chest- reportedly both his steel eyeglass case and his 50-page folded copy of the speech in his pocket maybe saved his life. Anyway, rather than...I don't know...*go to the hospital*, Roosevelt decided to give the speech anyway. He began his speech saying: "Friends, I shall ask you to be as quiet as possible. I don't know whether you fully understand that I have just been shot." He went on to finish that 90-minute speech before finally going to a hospital.

This election marked the first time New Mexico and Arizona participated in a Presidential election, as they both became states earlier that year. As election day drew near, things were not looking so good for Taft. To make matters worse, less than a week before the election, Vice President Sherman died. Sherman is the most recent Vice President to have died while in office.

And here are the results...

Woodrow Wilson won, becoming the twenty-eighth President in American history. Even though he had less votes than William Jennings Bryan ever had, he still easily won. He received 435 electoral votes, and 41.8% of the popular vote.

Coming in second was Teddy Roosevelt, who received 88 electoral votes and 27.4% of the popular vote. This was the last presidential election in which a candidate who was not a Republican or Democrat came in second place in either the Electoral College or popular vote. In third place, William Howard Taft, with just eight electoral votes and 23.2% of the popular vote. With so many former Republicans joining the Progressive Party, this resulted in the Republicans suffering their worst Presidential defeat in history. Taft suffered the worst ever defeat of any President trying to get reelected.

Interestingly, both Taft and Roosevelt lost their home states.

In fourth place, Eugene Debs got 6% of the popular vote. In fifth, Eugene Chafin got 1.4% of the popular vote.

Thomas Marshall became the twenty-eighth Vice President in American history.

Wilson would become the only Democrat President between 1896 and 1932, and only the second of two Democrats elected President between 1860 and 1932. Obviously, the Republican split had benefited him greatly, as he won several states that historically voted for the Republican candidate.

This election marked the only time since 1860 in which four different candidates each got more than 5% of the popular vote. Also, it was the only election in which a third party candidate did better than one of the major parties.

Again, now look at *this* map.

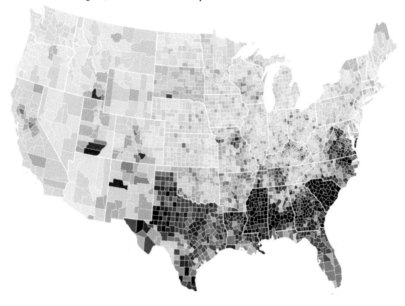

What the heck?

58.8% of the population voted in this election.

Turn the page for the next election, buddy.

The Presidential Election of 1916

vs.

Woodrow Wilson   **Charles Evans Hughes**

The thirty-third Presidential election in American history took place on November 7, 1916. Over in Europe, it pretty much seemed like the end of the world. Quite literally. The entire continent was destroying itself. Millions were mobilized and millions were dying in what later became known as World War One.

How horrifying was World War One? Well, to give you just a sample...The Battle of Verdun, which was still going on by election day, had been going on since February, still with no end in sight. In just this one battle, hundreds of thousands of soldiers had died. This was a new kind of war. One with industrialized weapons that could cause massive destruction, and one that simply the majority of Americans didn't want anything to do with.

Still, Americans had good reasons for not being too happy with the Germans. After a British ocean liner carrying Americans called the Lusitania was sunk by a German submarine the previous year, many had called for some kind of retaliation against the Germans.

At the same time, the Mexican Revolution was happening to the south, and people didn't know what was going to happen with their government. It was a truly scary time, but most Americans felt the United States should just stay neutral with foreign affairs. Let's just mind our own business, alright?

President Woodrow Wilson had kept the country neutral, and ran for reelection with the overwhelming support of the Democratic Party. Wilson and Vice President Thomas Marshall were easily renominated. The Democrats built their entire campaign around the slogan "He

Kept Us Out of War," scaring people into thinking that the Republicans would get the country in a war with both Germany and Mexico.

After suffering their worst Presidential defeat in history in 1912, the Republicans tried to rebound and heal the division that had caused the Progressives to leave. They went with the moderate and uncontroversial Charles Evans Hughes, who hadn't spoken publicly about political issues in six years because he was a Supreme Court Justice. Hughes was the only Supreme Court Justice to ever be nominated for President by a major political party. The Republicans nominated former Vice President Charles Fairbanks as his running mate, another safe choice.

The Progressive Party tried to renominate Theodore Roosevelt, but he turned it down, saying he didn't want to throw the election again to the Democrats. Because Roosevelt now just really wanted to see Wilson out of there, he endorsed Hughes, and many Progressives followed his lead. This left the Progressive Party in a mess, and they simply did not recover from this.

Meanwhile, the Socialist Party had to find someone else to run this time, as Eugene Debs was running for Congress instead this election. They nominated Allan Benson, a newspaper editor from Michigan, with George Ross Kirkpatrick, a political activist and writer from New Jersey, as his running mate. Both Benson and Kirkpatrick were very outspoken against getting involved with the war. In fact, they argued that all citizens should be able to vote by referendum whether to go to war or not.

The Prohibition Party nominated Frank Hanly, the former governor of Indiana, with Ira Landrith, a minister and activist from Tennessee, as his running mate.

Foreign policy dominated all of the campaigns. Wilson's people tried to promote the idea that he was the "peace candidate," despite the fact that Wilson had sent troops to intervene in the Mexican Civil War. Hughes just wanted the United States to be more ready to fight in case they had to.

And here are the results...

Woodrow Wilson won reelection, becoming the first Democrat to win two consecutive Presidential elections since Andrew Jackson. Wilson and Marshall were the first President and Vice President duo to be reelected since James Monroe and Daniel Tompkins back in 1820.

It was pretty close, though. The electoral vote was one of the closest in American history.

Wilson received 277 electoral votes, and Hughes received 254. In fact, the election was not called for several days, because everyone was waiting on California to deliver their results.

WIlson won California, but only by 3,800 votes. He got a solid 49.2% of the popular vote, though, and Hughes finished with 46.1%.

In third place, Allan Benson got 3.2% of the popular vote, and in fourth place, Frank Hanley, with 1.2%.

Hughes probably lost the election mainly because he failed to get all of the Progressives to come back to the Republican Party. Many still stubbornly refused.

Wilson won 200 counties that had never voted Democratic in a two-party contest prior to this election. While things were

looking up for the Democrats, they were not looking good for Wilson's promise for keeping the country out of war, as we will see on the next page.

61.6% of the population voted in this election.

Turn the page for the next election, buddy.

The Presidential Election of 1920

VS.

Warren Harding

James Cox

The thirty-fourth Presidential election in American history took place on November 2, 1920. Remember how Woodrow Wilson got reelected because he kept the country out of war? Well, before he was sworn in for his second term, it was looking like the United States would be entering World War One. The British had intercepted a telegram sent from Germany to Mexico trying to get Mexico to join their side in case the United States entered the war. Not only that, but Germany had begun unrestricted submarine warfare against *all* ships in the Atlantic Ocean bearing the American flag. Germany did this because Americans were exporting weapons to the Allies, who were their enemies, of course. Anyway, this got more Americans to change their minds about neutrality- more and more Americans now wanted to go to war. Wilson asked Congress to declare war on Germany in April 1917, and soon American troops were headed to Europe to aid the worn down French and British troops along the Western Front.

Woodrow Wilson wanted this to be the war to end all wars. Sounds good to me. The war ended with an armistice on November 11, 1918, and Wilson spent the remaining two years of his presidency trying to get peace agreements going to prevent something like this from ever happening again. He even had his statement of principles for world peace, which became known as the Fourteen Points.

Wilson worked tirelessly with the Allied leaders to help create the League of Nations, an alliance in which all the countries of the world could work together to work out their issues.

After the League of Nations was proposed as part of the Treaty of Versailles, Wilson went home to promote it and to try to get the United States to join and sign the treaty. I'll just go ahead and tell you- the United States never signed the Treaty of Versailles and never joined the

League of Nations. Congress couldn't get on board, and Wilson was not getting any love at all toward the end of his Presidency. Not only that, but Wilson suffered a series of horrible strokes that made him unable to do much during that time. His wife, Edith, pretty much ran things while Woodrow rested. This is why some half jokingly say she was the first female President of the United States.

Anyway, a ton of people wanted to take Wilson's spot to run for President. William Gibbs McAdoo, the former Treasury Secretary and Wilson's son-in-law, was a favorite, but Wilson blocked his nomination hoping that a deadlocked convention would cause *him* to get to run a third time, despite the fact that he was physically in terrible health. Instead, the Democrats chose James Cox, the Governor of Ohio and founder of a chain of newspapers that today has evolved into Cox Enterprises. They chose Franklin Roosevelt, the Assistant Secretary of the Navy, as his running mate. A big part of his appeal was name recognition, as he was a fifth cousin of Theodore Roosevelt, who had died the previous year.

The Republicans all of a sudden had a renewed interest in their party thanks to the backlash against the Treaty of Versailles, but they also had a hard time picking a candidate. Their convention was deadlocked between two candidates- Major General Leonard Wood and Frank Orren Lowden, the Governor of Illinois. Logically, the Republicans picked neither. Instead, in a smoke-filled room at the final hour, they picked Warren Harding, a U.S. Senator from Ohio. Harding was well-liked in his party because he never really did much to offend anybody. They nominated Calvin Coolidge, the Governor of Massachusetts, as Harding's running mate.

So essentially you had two dark horse candidates running against each other. Oh yeah, and third parties. How could I forget them?

Eugene Debs is back yet again. However, this time, he was in prison. That's right, Debs ran for President despite the fact that he was in prison for trying to get people to resist joining the draft during World War One. Deb talked a lot of trash against the Wilson administration for American involvement in the war, and Wilson called Debs a "traitor to his country." Debs was arrested and charged with sedition. He still had lots of supporters, though. The Socialist Party gets credit for nominating the first person for President to be locked in a prison cell. They chose a lawyer from Chicago named Seymour Stedman as his running mate.

Also, a new political party called the Farmer-Labor Party came to prominence this election pretty much because of the effect of American entry into the war, which hurt agricultural prices and worker wages. They were pretty much the Populist Party 2.0, nominating Parley Christensen, a former state representative from Utah, for President, and Max Hayes, a newspaper editor and activist from Ohio, as his running mate.

Despite the fact that Prohibition was now the law of the land with the passing of the 18th Amendment, the Prohibition Party was still around and nominated Aaron Watkins again for President. Seriously?

1919 and 1920 were absolutely crazy years in American history. There were riots and witch hunts and just a lot of paranoia and hatred going around. Not only that, there was a horrible pandemic killing hundreds of thousands of Americans.

Because of this, many Americans were drawn to the appeal of Warren Harding's "return to normalcy" campaign slogan, even though normalcy was before that an obscure math term and I think Harding meant to say "return to normality." They just wanted a return to the stability that was there before the war. Cox had a hard time distinguishing himself from Woodrow Wilson, and Wilson's popularity had fallen, especially since he was talking trash about immigrants. All of this, combined with the fact that the Harding campaign outspent the Cox campaign four to one, made things look promising again for the Republicans.

This was the first election since the ratification of the 19th Amendment, which gave women the right to vote. For the first time, women could vote for President in every state. It took long enough, dangit.

And here are the results...

Warren Harding easily won, becoming the twenty-ninth President in American history. It was a landslide. Harding received 404 electoral votes and 60.3% of the popular vote. Cox received just 127 electoral votes and only 34.2 % of the popular vote.

Eugene Debs, in his fifth and final presidential election, finished third again with 3.4% of the popular vote, and Parley Christensen finished fourth with 1% of the popular vote.

Calvin Coolidge became the twenty-ninth Vice President in American history.

Believe it or not, Harding became the first sitting U.S. Senator to ever be elected President.

How bad did Harding dominate in this election? Well, his popular vote victory is the second largest popular vote margin victory in a presidential election next only to the unopposed election of James Monroe in 1820, in the Era of Good Feelings. Man, this Harding dude must be amazing, right?

49.2% of the population voted in this election. With women now eligible to vote, voter turnout would be much lower, on average, in all elections after this one.

Turn the page for the next election, buddy.

The Presidential Election of 1924

Calvin Coolidge vs. John Davis vs. Robert La Follette

The thirty-fifth Presidential election in American history took place on November 4, 1924. Calvin Coolidge, the incumbent Republican President, was trying to stay in the White House. Wait a second, what happened to Harding?

Harding died from a heart attack in 1923, and so Coolidge took over. At the beginning of Harding's term, there had been a depression, but the economy quickly recovered, and now Coolidge was getting all the credit for it. The so-called Roaring Twenties were now in full swing, when everything seemed to become more modern and urban, and when American culture thrived at home and abroad.

Though Hiram Johnson, the U.S. Senator and former governor of California, challenged him, Calvin Coolidge was the Republican nominee. Charles Dawes, of the Dawes Plan fame, was his running mate.

William Gibbs McAdoo appeared again to be a favorite for the Democratic Party, at least early on. However, he had associated himself with Edward Doheny, a shady character who had become associated with the Teapot Dome scandal, which had tainted the Harding administration. As it turns out, Doheny associating with McAdoo really hurt McAdoo, among other things. Al Smith, the governor of New York, also looked to be a favorite. The Democratic National Convention was absolutely crazy. In fact, it was the longest ever. There were fist fights between McAdoo and Smith supporters, and the KKK kept coming up.

However, when it was all said and done, it was John Davis who got the nomination. As a compromise nominee, he didn't even give an acceptance speech.

Davis was fairly obscure. Some remembered him as a former U.S. Representative, or former U.S. Ambassador to the United Kingdom, or successful lawyer before that, but most people were like "who?" Davis was also a surprising choice to some because he was a fairly conservative, limited-government-type guy. The Democrats nominated Charles Wayland Bryan as his running mate. Bryan was William Jennings Bryan's younger brother and the governor of Nebraska.

Still, a lot of Americans were unsatisfied with the two-party system. Both Republicans and Democrats were associated with the Teapot Dome scandal, after all, and Coolidge and Davis seemed to be on the same page on a lot of issues.

For these Americans, Robert La Follette, the well known and by this time almost legendary U.S. Senator from Wisconsin, was the answer. A new political party was created that was centered around La Follette called the Progressive Party. No, not the Bull Moose Party of 1912, which La Follette actually opposed. This was a new Progressive Party that united the labor unions and farmers. La Follette fought hard during his entire career for things like child labor laws, a social security safety net, and ending Washington cronyism, and that now resonated with many in 1924. Burton Wheeler, a U.S. Senator from Montana, was La Follette's running mate.

As election day approached, things were looking really bad for the Democrats, as it appeared that many former Democrats were switching to support La Follette.

And here are the results...

Calvin Coolidge easily won, remaining the thirtieth President in American history. He received a dominating 382 electoral votes and 54% of the popular vote. John Davis finished second, receiving 136 electoral votes and only 28.8% of the popular vote. Davis's popular vote percentage is the lowest of any Democratic presidential candidate in American history, if you don't count the crazy election of 1860.

Robert La Follette finished third, receiving 13 electoral votes, which was just his home state of Wisconsin, and 16.6% of the popular vote. Was La Follette a spoiler? Well, he

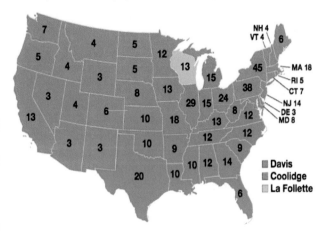

did mostly draw Democrats to his side, so yeah, you could argue that. However, he used to be a Republican, and it's safe to say he drew at least a few Republicans.

Charles Dawes became the thirtieth Vice President in American history.

And remember, Coolidge and Davis had agreed on many issues- both wanted limited government, less taxes, and fewer regulations. So La Follette was the only one to offer different views on several issues, but these were conservative times, baby. These were conservative times.

48.9% of the population voted in this election.

Turn the page for the next election, buddy.

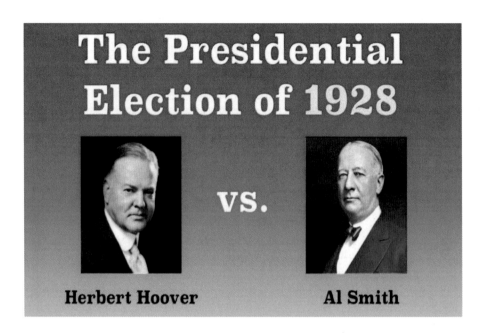

The Presidential Election of 1928

vs.

Herbert Hoover   **Al Smith**

The thirty-sixth Presidential election in American history took place on November 6, 1928, the day I turned negative 53. Calvin Coolidge had a smooth second term. The economy remained strong, and the federal government even had a huge surplus. If he wanted to run for another full term, he probably would have been easily reelected. However, Coolidge had announced the previous summer that he had no intention of running by cutting out strips of paper with the statement, "I do not choose to run for president in 1928" on them, and handing them out to reporters at the press conference. Coolidge said after the slips of paper were handed out, "There will be nothing more from this office today," and he walked out.

So this left the Republican nomination wide open. The leading candidates were Herbert Hoover, the Secretary of Commerce, Frank Orren Lowden, the former governor of Illinois, and the U.S. Senate Majority Leader Charles Curtis, who was from my home state of Kansas. Not impressed by these choices, many Republicans tried to draft Coolidge, but Coolidge turned it down. Hoover ended up getting the nomination, with Charles Curtis as his running mate.

The Democratic Party nominated Al Smith, the Governor of New York who was running for President a third time. Smith was the first Roman Catholic to be a major party's candidate for President. The Democrats nominated Joseph Taylor Robinson, a U.S. Senator from Arkansas and Senate Minority Leader, as his running mate. Robinson and Smith seemed like the odd couple, but actually complimented each other quite well.

No third parties really stood out during this election at all, and so we had another class two-way battle. Hoover had the momentum due to the fact that things were going pretty darn well overall in the country. In fact, at Hoover's nomination acceptance speech, he said, "We in

America today are nearer to the final triumph over poverty than ever before in the history of this land... We shall soon with the help of God be in sight of the day when poverty will be banished from this land."

Little did Hoover know that soon those words would come back to haunt him. However, things were looking pretty good for him, especially since Al Smith's religion became a major issue during the campaign. Many Protestants feared that Smith would take orders from the Pope if he led the country. In addition to anti-Catholicism, Smith's opposition to Prohibition and his association with the corruption of Tammany Hall likely would cost him votes.

And here are the results...

Herbert Hoover easily won, becoming the thirty-first President in American history. In the Electoral College, he dominated so much it was a bit embarrassing for the Democrats. Hoover received 444 electoral votes, and even won states like North Carolina and Virginia, which hadn't voted for a Republican for President since 1872. Al Smith received just 87 electoral votes.

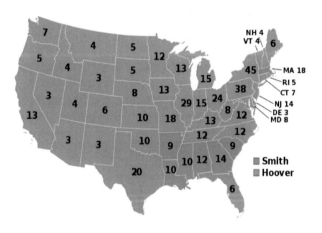

Hoover also dominated with the popular vote, getting 58.2% to Smith's 40.8%. It was safe to say the Republicans were on a roll, as this was their third consecutive presidential landslide victory.
Charles Curtis became the thirty-first Vice President in American history.

56.9% of the population voted in this election.

Turn the page for the next election, buddy.

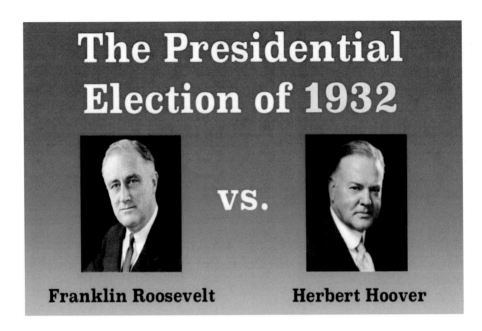

The Presidential Election of 1932

VS.

Franklin Roosevelt   **Herbert Hoover**

The thirty-seventh Presidential election in American history took place on November 8, 1932. A lot had changed since 1928. Herbert Hoover's time in office started out so promising, but on October 29, 1929, also known as Black Tuesday, the stock market crashed and triggered a bunch of events into motion that devastated economies around the entire world.

During the Hoover administration, industrial production shrank by 46%, wholesale prices dropped by 32%, and foreign trade shrank by 70%, while unemployment *increased* by 607%. One in four Americans couldn't find work, even though they often moved across the country, sometimes on foot, in order to find it. Personal income, tax revenue, and profits all dropped. The crime rate increased as unemployed workers often stole food to survive. Suicide rates and alcoholism rose. Marriages were delayed because many men wanted to wait until they could actually provide for a family. Less kids were born. It just sucked. It really, really sucked. Today we call this period of severe economic turmoil The Great Depression.

Hoover had the great misfortune of being in charge when this happened, and so therefore became a great scapegoat. It's not like he didn't try hard to stop it. He called for billions of dollars in taxpayer money for public works programs to create jobs. He called for stronger labor regulation laws. He called for the federal government bailing out struggling industries. To pay for this, he surprisingly called for more taxes. He raised tariffs by signing the Smoot-Hawley Tariff Act.

And many historians argue that by doing all of these things, Hoover was actually making the depression worse. Economists still argue about this today, but the bottom line is, in 1932 Hoover was not so popular. You could see this by the thousands of World War One veterans and their families camped out in Washington, D.C. demanding payments of a bonus that had been promised. Or the slums built by the poor people who couldn't find work that were nicknamed "Hoovervilles."

Hoover had grown to hate the presidency, but he didn't think any other Republican could do a better job than him, so he decided to run again. What's surprising is that the Republican Party overwhelmingly supported his renomination. Charles Curtis would also run again as Vice President. Kansas represent! Although, I should point out that he barely got renominated.

The Democratic Party seemed rejuvenated in 1932. They had three candidates competing for the nomination. Al Smith, the former governor of New York seeking the Presidency a fourth time, his friend but increasingly vocal critic Franklin Roosevelt, who was now the Governor of New York, and Speaker of the House John Nance Garner, who was from Texas. The Democrats went with Roosevelt, with Garner as his running mate.

There were many third parties, but only one really stood out much- the Socialist Party. They nominated Norman Thomas, a minister from New York. He also ran in 1928, but this time had growing support as so many Americans were unhappy with Hoover, yet also not satisfied with the Democrats. The Socialists nominated James Maurer, a trade unionist from Pennsylvania, as his running mate.

On the campaign trail, Hoover did his best to defend his record, but the odds were against him. Not only did many Americans blame Hoover for the Great Depression, most now were strongly against Prohibition, which was also associated with his administration. Roosevelt, who was not widely known before this election, was now a rock star, drawing huge crowds, inspiring hope that he had solutions to end the depression.

While Roosevelt didn't offer many specific solutions, he did get specific when criticizing Hoover. Roosevelt criticized the Smoot-Hawley Tariff and the Hoover administration for taxing and spending way too much. His running mate, Garner, went further, accusing Hoover of "leading the country down the path of socialism."

Toward the end of campaigning, things got downright nasty between the two, with Hoover calling Roosevelt a "chameleon in plaid" and Roosevelt calling Hoover a "fat, timid capon." A capon is a castrated rooster, by the way.

And here are the results...

No surprise here. Franklin Roosevelt won, becoming the thirty-second President in American history. He received 472 electoral votes and 57.4% of the popular vote. It was the first win for the Democrats since 1916, and an impressive one at that. Roosevelt received the highest percentage of the popular vote ever for a Democratic nominee up to that point. Hoover got just 59 electoral votes and 39.7% of the popular vote.

Norman Thomas finished third with 2.2% of the popular vote.

John Nance Garner, aka "Cactus Jack", became the thirty-second Vice President in American history.

This election was significant because it marked the beginning of 20 straight years of Democratic control of the White House. In fact, Democrats would be in office 28 out of the next 36 years. And get used to that name, Franklin Roosevelt. He's going to be around awhile.

52.6% of the population voted in this election.

Turn the page for the next election, buddy.

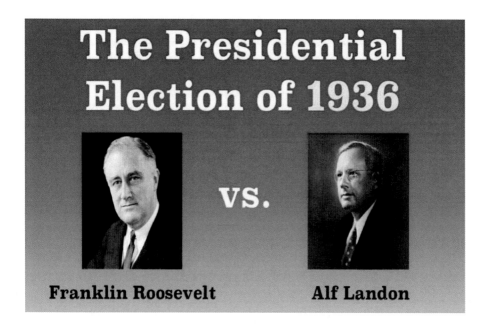

The Presidential Election of 1936

Franklin Roosevelt   VS.   Alf Landon

The thirty-eighth Presidential election in American history took place on November 3, 1936. Almost four years earlier, Franklin Roosevelt went straight to work, causing the federal government to become more involved with the economy than ever before. This was at a low point of the Great Depression, and Americans were desperate for any kind of positive news. They wanted the President to do something- *anything*, to try to help the economy, and Roosevelt, or FDR as we will call him from now on, gave executive orders and signed laws that were all meant to provide what historians call "The Three Rs." Those were relief for the unemployed and poor, recovery for the economy, and reform of the financial system so that a depression like this never happened again.

These laws and programs became famously known as The New Deal, and they are the reason why today we have things like social security, unemployment benefits, an eight-hour work day, a federal minimum wage, the FDIC, and the SEC.

FDR's New Deal was the federal government micromanaging at an unprecedented level, and in normal conditions, it probably wouldn't fly. But like I said, the people demanded action, and FDR delivered. While most Americans supported him, some did not, and the New Deal did not end the Depression. Some even argued it just prolonged it.

Just before the election, the Great Depression had entered its eighth year. FDR wanted four more years to more aggressively push for more New Deal programs. The New Deal had become very popular with the Democratic Party, and he was renominated with little opposition. Vice President John Nance Garner was once again his running mate.

My home state of Kansas dominated the Republican Party this election. While the party had many potential presidential nominees, only two stood out- Alf Landon, the former millionaire oilman and Governor of Kansas, and William Borah, a U.S. Senator from Idaho who had attended the University of Kansas. The party's establishment went with Landon, who actually supported many New Deal policies, yet had a strong reputation for being fiscally conservative and reducing taxes in Kansas. The Republicans nominated newspaper publisher Frank Knox as his running mate.

Louisiana Senator Huey Long, often nicknamed The Kingfish, had planned to run for President in 1936, but he was assassinated the year before, a month after he announced he was running actually. Like his friend Father Coughlin, a Roman Catholic priest who was a big radio star, Long had originally supported FDR in 1932, but later criticized him, saying he wasn't doing enough to help the poor. Long actually promoted the controversial Share Our Wealth program, which called for a massive redistribution of money from the super rich to everyone else.

After Long died, Coughlin pressed forward with the movement, which eventually turned into a new political party, called the Union Party. According to some historians, Coughlin and Long never wanted to win the 1936 election- they just wanted to split the progressive vote to cause FDR to lose. Regardless of whether or not this was true, the newly formed Union Party nominated William Lemke, a U.S. Representative from North Dakota who lacked charisma and a chance at winning this election. Thomas O'Brien, a lawyer from Boston, was his running mate.

Some political pundits predicted a close election, but the New Deal was very popular with many Americans, and with the Depression still dragging on many still kept their faith in it. Alf Landon was considered no match for FDR. Plus, he sucked at campaigning. Well actually, he *didn't* campaign. A columnist joked, "Considerable mystery surrounds the disappearance of Alfred M. Landon of Topeka, Kansas.... The Missing Persons Bureau has sent out an alarm bulletin bearing Mr. Landon's photograph and other particulars, and anyone having information of his whereabouts is asked to communicate direct with the Republican National Committee."

And here are the results...

Franklin Roosevelt destroyed Alf Landon. Not literally, of course, but look at the electoral map!

Talk about lopsided. This was the greatest electoral landslide since the beginning of the Democratic and Republican two-party system. FDR received 523 electoral votes, and Landon received eight. No, you didn't mishear that. Eight electoral votes, which was two states-Vermont and Maine. This was the biggest electoral victory ever, unless you count the uncontested election of 1820 or the George Washington elections.

FDR won 60.8% of the popular vote, compared to Landon getting just 36.5%. Again, not counting 1820 or the George Washington elections, this was the second highest popular-vote percentage in American history, next only to the election of 1964.

William Lemke finished third, with 2% of the popular vote.

You might say it was an embarrassing loss for Landon. Before the election, some polls had predicted Landon would win. Oops. However, one advertising executive named George Gallup conducted a scientific poll that predicted FDR would win. His correct prediction made public opinion polling more important in future elections, and today we have The Gallup Poll, named after him. So the New Deal continued, as it probably would have anyway. Unfortunately, so did the Great Depression.

56.9% of the population voted in this election.

Turn the page for the next election, buddy.

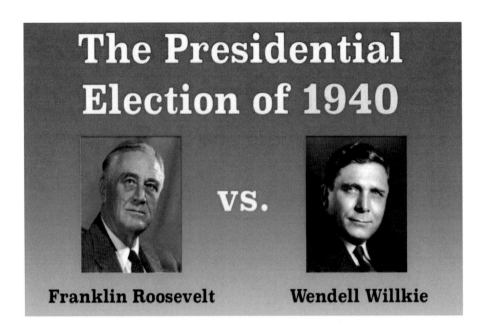

The Presidential Election of 1940

VS.

Franklin Roosevelt   **Wendell Willkie**

The thirty-ninth Presidential election in American history took place on November 5, 1940. The Great Depression dragged on, and now another world war was being fought all across Europe and in Asia. Franklin Roosevelt, or FDR, had remained popular despite the fact that his New Deal policies had become increasingly liberal, for lack of a better word, and despite the fact he tried to pack the Supreme Court so that more of his New Deal policies would not be struck down as unconstitutional.

While the economy had shown signs of recovering early in FDR's second term, it suddenly went downhill again soon after that. Some former FDR supporters began to lose faith in him. Former allies were now enemies. Al Smith, for example, constantly criticized FDR and had even supported Alf Landon for the 1936 election.

After the Supreme Court packing attempt, Vice President John Nance Garner turned against FDR, and said he would run for President in 1940. That didn't seem to stop the majority of the country from supporting Roosevelt, which was why there were rumours that he might try for an unprecedented third term. FDR had told several people he had no intention of running again, as that would break the two-term tradition set by George Washington 144 years prior. His wife, Eleanor, said he shouldn't do it.

At the Democratic National Convention, Garner and FDR's former campaign manager and the Postmaster General James Farley were the two leading candidates for the nomination. But enough key people influenced the majority that only FDR could keep the New Deal policies going, and it was he who once again got the nomination, with Henry Wallace, the Secretary of Agriculture, as his running mate this time.

The Republican Party, who some said would die after the embarrassing defeat of Alf Landon in the 1936 presidential election, found new life when in 1938 they gained a lot of seats in Congress. The downturn of the economy certainly sparked this. By 1940, they thought they were ready to take FDR down.

Still, the party was divided between the interventionists, those who wanted to become more actively involved in what became known as World War Two, and the non-interventionists, who were those who wanted to stay out of the war. Three Republican candidates stood out. Robert Taft, the son of former President and Supreme Court Chief Justice William Howard Taft and a U.S. Senator from Ohio, was a non-interventionist. Arthur Vandenberg, a U.S. Senator from Michigan, who leaned a bit non-interventionist, and Thomas Dewey, the District Attorney of New York county, who leaned a bit more interventionist than the other two but was still a non-interventionist. Dewey got the most votes early on but was criticized for his youth and lack of foreign policy experience.

All three candidates had weaknesses, actually, and only 300 of the 1,000 delegates had been pledged to a candidate by the time of the Republican National Convention. This left an opening for a dark horse. That dark horse had a really cool name. Wendell Willkie, a lawyer, businessman, and former Democrat who had never previously run for public office. Wilkie had a passionate core of supporters who won most the rest of the Republicans over. Interestingly enough, Wilkie was somewhat of an interventionist. The Republicans nominated Charles McNary, the Senate Minority Leader, as his running mate, even though McNary had tried to block Willkie's nomination at the convention.

No third parties stood out at all during this election.

Unlike Landon in 1936, Willkie aggressively attacked FDR. While he was ok with having New Deal welfare programs, he talked trash about how they were poorly run and created great uncertainty for businesses. He argued the country was not prepared for war, yet, at the same time, Roosevelt was leading the country down the path to war. He also questioned why FDR was breaking the two-term presidential tradition to begin with.

However, Big Business was still mostly blamed at this time for the Depression, and Willkie couldn't escape being associated with that. Because Willkie campaigned everywhere he could, sometimes he was heckled by crowds. He often had rotten fruit and vegetables thrown at him.

And here are the results...

Franklin Roosevelt became the first and only President in American history to be elected for a third term. He received 449 electoral votes, in another landslide victory. He also dominated the popular vote, getting 54.7%

Wendell Willkie finished with 82 electoral votes and 44.8% of the popular vote.

Henry Wallace became the thirty-third Vice President in American history.

There was strong contrast between urban and rural this election. Americans in the big cities mostly tended to support FDR, while Americans in smaller cities and in rural areas mostly tended to support Willkie.

58.8% of the population voted in this election.

Turn the page for the next election, buddy.

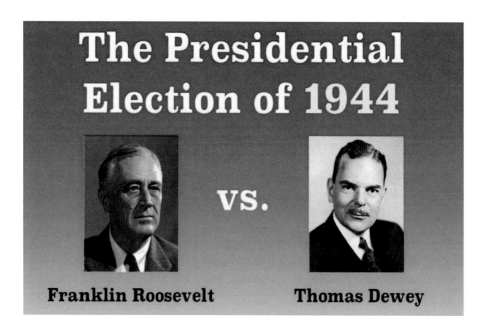

The Presidential Election of 1944

vs.

Franklin Roosevelt   **Thomas Dewey**

The fortieth Presidential election in American history took place on November 7, 1944. Almost three years earlier, the Empire of Japan attacked an American naval base at Pearl Harbor, Hawaii. 2400 Americans were killed and 1200 wounded. The attack also damaged five battleships, three destroyers, and seven other ships and more than 200 aircraft were ruined. It completely took most Americans by surprise, and the next day President Franklin Roosevelt asked Congress to declare war on Japan, which they promptly did. Soon after, the United States also found itself at war with Nazi Germany, joining the struggling Allies. This war became known as World War Two, and uh...*it's the biggest war of all time.*

By election day 1944, the war was going much better for the Allies, as the forces of both Japan and Germany had severely weakened. Roosevelt, or FDR, had become a popular war time President. Unlike in 1940, he did not hesitate to run for reelection during this very critical time. The Democratic Party mostly supported him, and he was renominated. However, most conservative Democrats were uneasy about renominating Vice President Henry Wallace, who they argued was too friendly with labor unions and those wanting to end racial segregation in the South. Some recommended Harry Truman, the U.S. Senator from Missouri, who seemed to be more moderate. Truman had made a name for himself fighting fraud and waste in the war program, but FDR didn't know him very well. FDR trusted and liked Wallace, but gave in to the pressure from the Democratic Party to have Truman be his running mate instead.

Even with Truman's nomination, several conservative Democrats were not happy. For years, they had not liked the way both the New Deal and the war effort expanded the size of the federal government and hurt business. After the Supreme Court decision Smith v. Allwright, which said a Texas law saying it was ok to discriminate against African Americans in

Democratic Party primaries was unconstitutional, they became even more upset with FDR and the party establishment. This group became known as the Texas Regulars, and they ended up breaking away from the Democrats. They were purely a protest group, and they never even could agree on another candidate. Their main goal was to prevent the reelection of FDR.

The Republicans again had many folks interested in their presidential nomination. Wendell Willkie was interested again. Thomas Dewey was interested again. Robert Taft was not. Instead, he told everyone that John Bricker, the Governor of Ohio, would make a fine president. But some former Taft supporters gravitated toward General Douglas MacArthur, who was then leading Allied forces in the Pacific theater of the war. Another leading contender for the nomination was Harold Stassen, who ran for President pretty much every four years for the rest of the century. I'm exaggerating, of course. He had been the governor of Minnesota when he decided to give up the position to fight the war in the Pacific as a naval officer.

Well, this time the Republicans went with Dewey, who by this time was the Governor of New York had become more of a national figure anyway. They chose Bricker as his running mate. It was a fairly strong ticket, but interestingly enough, Wendell Willkie, the Republican nominee of 1940, had not endorsed them. In fact, Willkie had been pretty friendly to FDR since the last election, and some even speculated that Willkie could have been FDR's new running mate instead of Truman. No one would find out what he was truly thinking, however, because Willkie died of a heart attack on October 8. 1944.

On the campaign trail, Dewey talked trash about how FDR needed to lay off the economy and shrink the size of government, now that the end of the war was in sight. FDR argued he was just doing whatever was necessary to win the war, and most Americans generally agreed with him. There was one issue- some doubted FDR could make it another term, as his health appeared to be on the decline. Because of this, the Democrats had to sell his running mate, Harry Truman.

And here are the results....

FDR won, becoming the first and only President in American history to be elected for a fourth term. He dominated yet another election, receiving 432 electoral votes and 53.4% of the popular vote.

Thomas Dewey finished second with 99 electoral votes and 45.9% of the popular vote. Don't worry, he'd be back.

Harry Truman became the thirty-fourth Vice President in American history. FDR's decision to go with him proved to be pretty important, as Roosevelt died the next April, less than three months after beginning his fourth term. It was Truman, not Henry Wallace, who would become the country's thirty-third President.

Within a few years, the Constitution would be amended to prevent presidents from ever serving more than two terms, mostly because of FDR getting elected four times.

56.1% of the population voted in this election.

Turn the page for the next election, buddy.

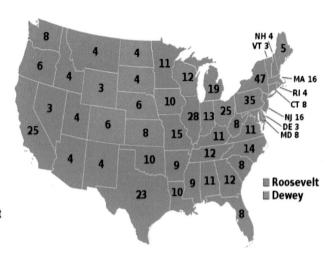

NH 4
VT 3
5
MA 16
RI 4
CT 8
NJ 16
DE 3
MD 8

8
4
4
11
6
4
3
4
12
19
47
35
3
6
10
25
28 13
25
8 11
4
6
8
15
11
14
12
4
4
10
9
8
9 11 12
23
10
8

Roosevelt
Dewey

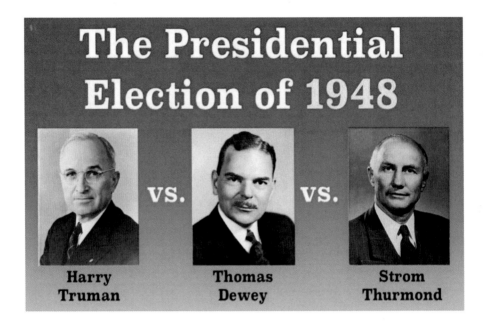

The Presidential Election of 1948

Harry Truman vs. **Thomas Dewey** vs. **Strom Thurmond**

The forty-first Presidential election in American history took place on November 2, 1948. After Franklin Roosevelt died, Harry Truman took over as President, and soon after Nazi Germany surrendered to the Allied forces. Now, all eyes were on the Pacific theater of the war. Japan was clearly suffering, but it didn't seem like they were going to surrender anytime soon. I mean, Japanese pilots were conducting suicide attacks, known as kamikaze, aimed at warships.

While some historians debate whether or not the Japanese government was actually ready to surrender in the summer of 1945, Truman took action and decided to drop the first and only atomic bombs ever dropped on another country. He did it to end the war quickly and try to save the lives of millions of both Americans and Japanese who would have kept on fighting otherwise. While today people still debate whether or not the action was justified, it's hard to deny how bold the move was by Truman, and it worked. Japan finally surrendered shortly after Americans dropped two atomic bombs on Hiroshima and Nagasaki. The war was over, and this time Truman made it a point to not make the same mistakes that were made after World War One.

Instead of punishment, Truman called for aid. He pushed for the Marshall Plan, which had Americans give money to Western European countries to help them rebuild their economies after the war. They would also help rebuild Japan.

Truman's presidency was a huge turning point for world affairs. Sure, World War Two was over, but now he was all about fueling the Cold War with the Soviet Union. Truman was cold with Joseph Stalin the moment he took over, and some argue he helped start the Cold War with his strained relationship with the Soviet dictator. Who could blame him, though. It's not like Stalin was a lovable kitty cat or anything. Truman's foreign policy objectives became famously known as the Truman Doctrine, with the main objective being always to defeat Communism, wherever it appeared. Truman called for aid to resistance movements in Turkey and Greece where communist revolutions threatened, and he supported the Berlin Airlift, which of course made the Soviet Union even more upset with the United States.

Back home, Truman was the first President to actively call for civil rights legislation. He even desegregated the armed forces. I've read several quotes by Truman that are pretty racist, and maybe he just did this to get the black vote, but man this was a huge step in 1948.

Anyway, after all this Truman had a very low approval rating- it seemed not nearly as many Americans liked him like they did FDR. Not only that, several people in his own political party were turning against him. They tried to get Dwight Eisenhower, the World War Two hero and former Chief of Staff of the United States Army, to be the nominee instead of Truman. But they failed, as Eisenhower refused to run. Eventually the Democrats went ahead and went with Truman as their nominee, with Alben Barkley, the Senate Minority Leader, as his running mate.

Though Truman tried to moderate his civil rights positions, some Democrats were like "nuh-uh" and walked out of the Democratic Convention. They started a new political party, called the States' Rights Democratic Party. Members of this party became known as Dixiecrats. The Dixiecrats wanted to keep the policy of racial segregation in the South and allow states to keep their infamous Jim Crow laws. They nominated Strom Thurmond, the Governor of South Carolina and the guy who led the walkout of the Democratic convention, for President, and Fielding Wright, the Governor of Mississippi, as his running mate. Fielding Wright? More like Fielding Wrong. Ha! Sorry, bad joke.

Anyway, it wasn't just the Dixiecrats who left the Democratic Party. Some Democrats argued that Truman's civil rights reforms didn't do enough for blacks. They wanted more. Former Vice President Henry Wallace, who...remember, would have been President if it weren't for Truman taking his place in the 1944 election, disagreed with Truman on many issues. In fact, Truman had fired Wallace from his position as the Secretary of Commerce after Wallace talked trash about Truman's foreign policy. Wallace opposed the Truman Doctrine and wanted to get rid of the House Un-American Activities Committee, which he thought violated civil liberties. Wallace also called for more regulation against giant corporations and an expanded welfare state. Naturally, opponents called him a secret Communist.

Wallace and his supporters also left the Democratic Party to form a third Progressive Party, called the...um...Progressive Party. Can't we get more creative with names, folks? Again, this was not the same Progressive Party as Teddy Roosevelt (Bull Moose Party) or Robert La Follette- it was a new one. This Progressive Party officially nominated Wallace as their nominee, with Glen Taylor, a U.S. Senator from Idaho, as his running mate. Taylor had earned a reputation as being that one weird politician in DC. A guy known as the "singing cowboy" because he would sing songs and ride his horse up the steps of the Capitol. To be fair, he didn't sing songs and ride his horse up the steps at the same time.

So Wallace and Taylor were definitely unique. When they campaigned, they made a point of speaking to racially integrated audiences, even in the South, and because of that, Southerners sometimes threw food like eggs and tomatoes at them.

Oh no! I spent so much time talking about Democrats and former Democrats that I almost forgot about the Republicans. Well, they tried for Dwight Eisenhower, too, but after Eisenhower declined, many familiar names stood out for the nomination. Thomas Dewey, Robert Taft, Arthur Vandenburg, and Harold Stassen, who were all in the running in 1944. However, there were also some who didn't run in 1944. Notably, there was Earl Warren, the Governor of California (and a future Supreme Court Chief Justice). The Republicans decided to play it safe and go once again with Thomas Dewey, who was still Governor of New York. They nominated Warren as his running mate.

Dewey and Warren, as governors of two of the largest states in the country, made up a strong ticket. And with the Democratic Party fractured, nearly every poll favored them to win. Dewey made sure he did whatever he could to just avoid major mistakes- he often was vague on policy and in speeches. As I said before, Truman was not a popular President and even had a hard time raising money for his campaign. Shortly before election day, journalists were so confident that Dewey would win that they went ahead and wrote articles ahead of time proclaiming him as the next President.

And here are the results...

Dewey won. Just kidding! In what is considered to be perhaps the greatest election upset in American history, Harry Truman won, remaining the thirty-third President in American history. No one seemed to see this one coming, and yet Truman had won by more than two million votes.

He sure had some fun holding up this newspaper.

Truman received 303 electoral votes and 49.6% of the popular vote. Thomas Dewey received 189 electoral votes and 45.1% of the popular vote.

As expected, Strom Thurmond did well in the South. He received 39 electoral votes, but just 2.4% of the popular vote.

While he didn't receive any electoral votes, Henry Wallace received a solid 2.4% of the popular vote as well, getting just under 19,000 votes less than Thurmond for fourth place.

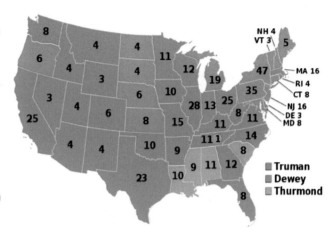

Alben Barkley became the thirty-fifth Vice President in American history.

The election of 1948 will forever be known as the underdog election, inspiring future candidates who were behind in the polls that they always had a chance.

51.1% of the population voted in this election.

Turn the page for the next election, buddy.

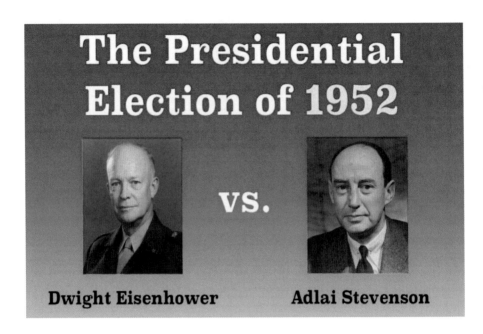

The Presidential Election of 1952

Dwight Eisenhower   VS.   **Adlai Stevenson**

The forty-second Presidential election in American history took place on November 4, 1952. Oh Harry. Harry Truman had managed to get the country into another war. But now the United States military was acting as the leading force for an organization he had helped start, called the United Nations. United Nations forces arrived to help defend South Korea after Communist North Korea invaded them. This was back in 1950. Two years later, the conflict dragged on as a stalemate. Truman called it just a "police action," but today we know it as the Korean War. Even though the war still gets glossed over, tens of thousands of Americans died in it, and Truman's popularity declined the longer that it continued.

Senator Joseph McCarthy's anti-Communist attacks and the revelation of widespread corruption of federal employees also hurt Truman's approval rating, so much that he hesitated to run for reelection. He cautiously proceeded, though, trying to talk Adlai Stevenson II to run. Stevenson was the Governor of Illinois and grandson of former Vice President Adlai Stevenson I. However, Stevenson resisted running, and the populist Estes Kefauver, a U.S. Senator from Tennessee, became a leading candidate. After Kefauver upset Truman in the New Hampshire primary, Truman dropped out. Kefauver continued to win many primaries, but powerful people within the Democratic Party establishment simply thought he was too much of an outsider, and therefore could not be trusted. At the Democratic National Convention, Kefauver was the early favorite, but eventually the party's bosses were able to convert enough people to support Adlai Stevenson, who finally was like, "alright, fine. I'll run. Sure." They nominated John Sparkman, a U.S. Senator from Alabama, as his running mate. This was mostly because they wanted the former Dixiecrats back, as Sparkman was alright with racial segregation.

The Republican Party had a four-way race for the nomination. Dwight Eisenhower, the World War Two hero, had finally been persuaded to run for President, and he had three familiar opponents- Robert Taft, Earl Warren, and Harold Stassen. Because Warren and Stassen only won the primaries in their home states, this was really more of a two-way race between Eisenhower and Taft. The two had quite different foreign policies. Taft was a non-interventionist, criticizing the Korean War and calling for less involvement in foreign conflicts. Eisenhower was cool with the Truman Doctrine, seeing the spread of Communism as a big threat that needed to be stopped whenever possible. Taft also criticized Truman for the welfare state that had ballooned since the New Deal, while Eisenhower was cool with keeping the welfare state.

Eisenhower and Taft were neck and neck in the primary race. Going into the Republican convention- everyone knew it would be one of those two. But Taft's campaign got accused of silencing Eisenhower delegates from Southern states. Whether true or not, this ended up hurting Taft. After a bitter and divided convention, Eisenhower barely came out as the winner, with Richard Nixon, a U.S. Senator from California, as his running mate, who accused others of being crooks (calling out corruption in government), and some accused him of being a crook (taking campaign money he wasn't supposed to), but he cleared everything up with a dramatic speech where he mentioned his dog Checkers.

Even though he barely got the nomination, Eisenhower was an incredibly popular candidate thanks to being a war hero, and he drew huge crowds. He was way ahead in the polls throughout his campaign, and even had a catchy slogan, "I Like Ike." Adlai Stevenson drew big crowds, too, but he became famously known as an "egghead," not only because of his baldness, but because of his tendency of coming across as too intellectual and out of touch with ordinary people.

Both campaigns used television ads quite a bit, marking a shift that many people actually had them now. Toward the end of his campaign, Eisenhower announced he would look at ending the Korean War and bringing the troops home.

And here are the results...

Dwight Eisenhower easily won, becoming the thirty-fourth President in American history. Promising to bring the troops home from Korea provided the final boost he needed to handily win it. He received 442 electoral votes and 55.2% of the popular vote.

Adlai Stevenson finished second with just 89 electoral votes and 44.3% of the popular vote. The Democrats had lost control of the executive branch for the first time in twenty years.

Ike did well everywhere except the Deep South.

Richard Nixon became the thirty-sixth Vice President in American history.

This was the first election in which a computer predicted the results, and for some reason, turnout soared compared to the last election.

61.6% of the population voted in this election.

Turn the page for the next election, buddy.

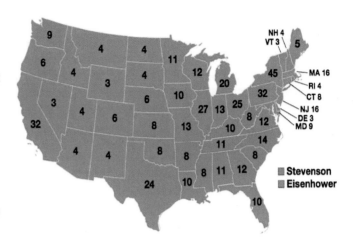

NH 4
VT 3
5
MA 16
RI 4
CT 8
NJ 16
DE 3
MD 9

9
4
4
11
6
4
3
4
12
20
45
32
3
6
10
27
13
25
32
32
4
6
8
13
10
8
12
4
4
8
8
11
14
8
8
11
12
24
10
10

■ Stevenson
■ Eisenhower

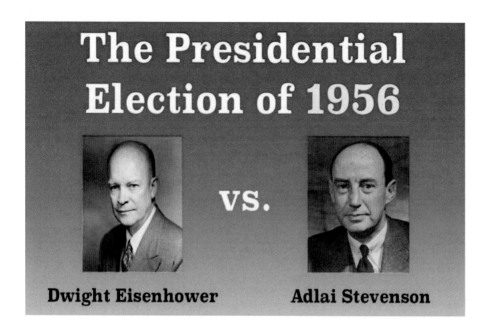

The Presidential Election of 1956

VS.

Dwight Eisenhower   **Adlai Stevenson**

The forty-third Presidential election in American history took place on November 6, 1956, the day I turned negative 25. Uh-oh, we got a re-match! Dwight Eisenhower remained very popular, and his first term went fairly well, except for having a heart attack. But he had recovered from that, and decided for a second term. He was easily renominated without opposition. Vice President Richard Nixon, even if he was a bit more polarizing than Eisenhower, was also easily renominated. Eisenhower had brought the troops home from Korea and the economy remained strong. He had proven to be a strong Cold War leader as well, and he helped many Americans feel safe again. It was going to be hard for *anyone* to run against him.

But the Democrats tried anyway. Adlai Stevenson, the now former governor of Illinois who ran for President and lost in 1952, decided to give it another go against Eisenhower. However, Estes Kefauver returned to challenge him, and did surprisingly well in early primaries. Stevenson welcomed the challenge, and the two participated in the very first nationally televised presidential debate before the Florida primary. In Florida, Stevenson won a close contest, and from there he had the momentum. Stevenson ended up winning the nomination again, but to get everyone fired up he decided to let the delegates choose his running mate at the Democratic convention. This made the convention pretty darn exciting, and a young U.S. Senator from Massachusetts by the name of John Kennedy got a lot of buzz. However, the Democratic Party delegates ultimately went with Kefauver as Stevenson's running mate.

Stevenson campaigned vigorously against Eisenhower. He called for getting rid of the draft, lowering military spending, ending nuclear bomb testing (which was kind of getting out of control), and expanding social programs for the needy. As things were going pretty well for the country, Eisenhower campaigned on his record, and he won the support of many African

Americans with his support of the Brown v. Board of Education Supreme Court ruling, which said racial segregation in public schools was unconstitutional.

This was the first election in which television ads dominated each campaign. Who knew that video could be such an effective medium?

And here are the results...

Dwight Eisenhower easily won reelection, winning by an even larger margin than he did in 1952. He received 457 electoral votes. Adlai Stevenson only received 73 electoral votes this time. He won Alabama, but one faithless elector there randomly voted for Walter Burgwyn Jones, a judge from the state. Thanks, 1956 election, for reminding us why the Electoral College is flawed.

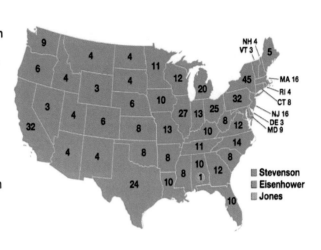

As for the popular vote, Eisenhower got 57.4% and Stevenson got just 42%.

This was the last presidential election that was an exact rematch of an election held four years prior.

59.3% of the population voted in this election.

Turn the page for the next election, buddy.

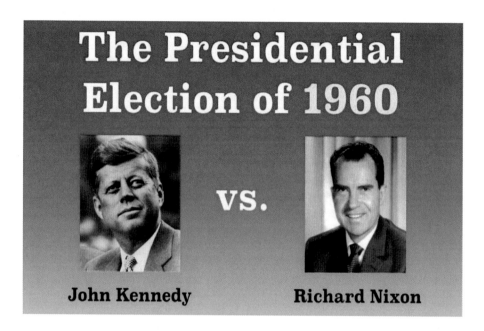

The Presidential Election of 1960

John Kennedy

VS.

Richard Nixon

The forty-fourth Presidential election in American history took place on November 8, 1960. It was the first election in which Alaska and Hawaii could both participate. Dwight Eisenhower had a pretty good run, but he was the first President officially not allowed to seek a third term. His Vice President for eight years, Richard Nixon, now enthusiastically sought the Presidency. Several Republicans, however, supported Nelson Rockefeller, the Governor of New York and member of the wealthy Rockefeller family. Rockefeller was the leader of the liberal/moderate wing of the Republican Party.

After Rockefeller decided to drop out of the race, Nixon easily won the Republican nomination, but he was a little worried he didn't have the Rockefeller Republicans on his side, so he met with him to make sure they were on the same page on many issues. By doing this, Nixon sort of officially became a big government Republican, you could say. Henry Cabot Lodge, Jr., the U.S. Ambassador to the United Nations, was Nixon's running mate. Lodge was a familiar name, as he was the grandson of Senator Henry Cabot Lodge and also had a bunch of other ancestors who were involved with national politics.

The Democrats knew they had to nominate someone exciting to get back to the White House. Many Democrats were interested in being the nominee. Most of them were new to the national scene, but most were just not that exciting. Pat Brown, the Governor of California, wanted the nomination, but he wasn't that exciting. Stuart Symington, a U.S. Senator from Missouri, wanted it and was a bit more exciting. Then there was Adlai Stevenson, who had lost the last two presidential elections. As it turns out, he was not exciting, especially since with him it was "been there, done that." Wayne Morse, a U.S. Senator from Oregon. Ah, that's better. Lyndon Johnson, the Senate Majority Leader. Well that's even better. Hubert Humphrey, a U.S. Senator from Minnesota? Yeah, he got people fired up a bit. But really, there was just one man that energized the Democratic Party far more than any other, and that was John Kennedy. Despite some harsh criticism that he was too young to be President–he was just 43 after all–the Democratic Party went with him anyway.

Even though Kennedy and Lyndon Johnson had their disagreements, Kennedy helped unite the party behind him by asking Johnson to be his running mate, and Johnson accepted.

So it was Nixon versus Kennedy. Both of them drew huge, enthusiastic crowds everywhere they went. Nixon promised to campaign in all 50 states, even Alaska and Hawaii. He probably later regretted that promise, however, after he hurt his knee on a car door and the knee got severely infected. After he recovered two weeks later, he stayed true to his pledge, but some historians say he was an idiot for doing so, as he likely just wasted valuable time visiting states he had no chance of winning anyway.

Lyndon Johnson greatly helped Kennedy by aggressively campaigning in the South. It was actually quite a smart move for Kennedy to choose him as his running mate. Still, several Americans criticized Kennedy for his youth, and just like with Al Smith in 1928, there were plenty of Protestants who didn't want Kennedy, a Roman Catholic, as President because of his religion.

Since the economy was strong, Kennedy and Nixon often attacked each other on foreign policy. Believe it or not, this was the first time live presidential debates were held in the general election. There were four of them, and they were all on television, so it was a pretty big deal. For the first debate, most people who listened to it on the radio agreed that Nixon won. However, for those who saw it on TV, most agreed that *Kennedy* won. Why? Many say that Nixon looked uncomfortable and weak. He kept sweating, and was still recovering from his recent knee injury. He was tired from campaigning all day, and hadn't worn any  makeup, so his beard stubble showed up to viewers at home. Meanwhile, Kennedy looked rested, tan, and confident during the debate. It's pretty crazy how many agree that appearing on television literally changed the outcome of this election.

However, going into election day, it was difficult to predict who would win. Everyone knew it would be close, and therefore this election became one of the most suspenseful and dramatic in American history.

And here are the results...

In an absolute squeaker, John Kennedy won, becoming the thirty-fifth President in American history. It was the closest presidential election since 1916. How close? Well, in Nixon's home state of California, Kennedy appeared to win by 37,000 votes. However, after absentee ballots were counted a week later, Nixon came back to win the state by 36,000 votes.

As with many close elections, the losing side accused the winning side of voting fraud, especially in Illinois and Texas, where it was especially close. If Nixon would have won those two states, he would have won the election.

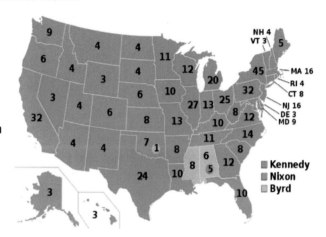

When it was all said and done, Kennedy received 303 electoral votes and Nixon received 219 electoral votes. 14 unpledged Democratic electors won election from voters in Mississippi and Alabama. In other words, these were protest votes against Kennedy for his support of the civil rights movement. Instead, they cast their votes for Harry Byrd, a U.S. Senator from Virginia. Byrd also got another electoral vote in Oklahoma from an elector who broke his promise that he'd vote for Nixon. All of this didn't matter, though, as these electors didn't change the outcome of the election.

The popular vote was obviously much closer. Kennedy got 49.7% and Nixon got 49.6%. Just 112,827 votes separated the two.

Lyndon Johnson became the thirty-seventh Vice President in American history.

At 43 years old, Kennedy became the youngest person ever elected President.

62.8% of the population voted in this election.

Turn the page for the next election, buddy.

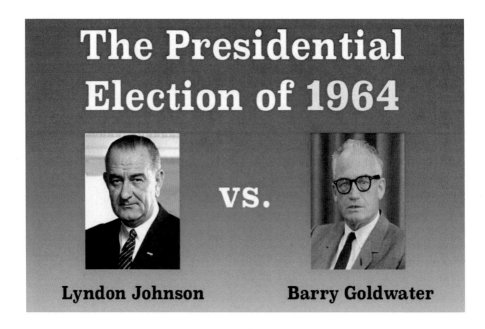

The Presidential Election of 1964

vs.

Lyndon Johnson   **Barry Goldwater**

The forty-fifth Presidential election in American history took place on November 3, 1964. Almost a full year before this, John F. Kennedy was assassinated while visiting Dallas, Texas, leaving the nation shocked and heartbroken. Vice President Lyndon Johnson was sworn in, becoming the thirty-sixth President in American history.

Lyndon Johnson sought to carry on many of Kennedy's policies, but he was certainly no Kennedy. One thing probably was different- many argue Kennedy would have handled the escalation of sending troops to Vietnam to fight the Communist Viet Cong differently than Johnson. Although Kennedy was the one who started sending troops there, some argue that right before he died he had wanted to withdraw- to bring the troops home. Johnson, on the other hand, ended up staying the course and sending *more* troops to Vietnam. In fact, his administration pretty much made up the fact that American navy ships were attacked twice by North Vietnam, in what became known as the Gulf of Tonkin incident. After this, Congress gave President Johnson the authority, without a declaration of war, to do whatever possible to help South Vietnam fight back against North Vietnam. This became known as the Vietnam War.

Overall, though, Johnson had aligned himself with Kennedy, and therefore was popular. He and most others were confident the Democratic Party would nominate him for President again, but he did face some challenges revolving around the civil rights movement. Earlier that year, Johnson had signed the Civil Rights Act, which gave the federal government power to enforce ending discrimination based on skin color, religion, gender, or national origin.

First of all, there were the Dixiecrats, who never really went away since 1948. They obviously didn't like the Civil Rights Act so much. Led by George Wallace, the Governor of Alabama, many of them threatened to leave the Democratic Party for good and even become Republicans. Wallace, who was totally against racial integration (aka for segregation), actually did fairly well in the Democratic primaries, even in some northern states like Wisconsin, Indiana, and Maryland. Other than that, "favorite son" candidates, or ones who were popular where they came from, dominated the Democratic primaries. They all had ulterior motives, however, as they were just going to give their votes to Lyndon Johnson.

So Lyndon Johnson got the nomination, and the Democrats nominated Hubert Humphrey, the U.S. Senator from Minnesota, as his running mate. However, there was a major controversy at the Democratic Convention when the Mississippi Freedom Democratic Party, made up of mostly African Americans who challenged the all-white Mississippi delegation who were elected in a shady way so that there would be no black delegates, protested. A compromise was reached to give more black representation, but many white delegates refused to compromise and they walked out of the convention.

Not only that, but Johnson and Robert Kennedy, the popular brother of John Kennedy and the Attorney General, did not like each other. Most Democrats wanted Kennedy as Johnson's new running mate, but Johnson turned him down. In fact, Johnson had the FBI monitor Kennedy and made sure he spoke on the last day of convention to make sure he wasn't drafted by delegates to be his running mate.

Despite all this, Johnson was a huge favorite to win, because Barry Goldwater was his opponent.

Other than his foreign policy views, Goldwater was a bit of a libertarian-type guy. Goldwater became the Republican nominee after a tough fight with Nelson Rockefeller, the Governor of New York. After Richard Nixon had declared he would not run for President this time, a bunch of Republicans, including even a woman, sought the Republican nomination. But Barry and Nelson were the two leading candidates, with Nelson representing the more moderate to liberal Republicans and Barry representing the more conservative. At the Republican convention, there was a lot of trash talking and a lot of booing, but ultimately Goldwater got the nomination, with William Miller, an obscure U.S. Representative from New York, as his running mate.

Barry Goldwater freaked a bunch of Republicans out, so much that they couldn't support him and instead pledged to vote for Johnson. Opponents of Goldwater called him a "radical" and "extremist." It didn't help that leaders of the KKK supported him. Because Goldwater wanted to be more aggressive in Vietnam and in fighting proxy wars against the Soviet Union in general, the Johnson campaign successfully freaked people out with what became known as the "Daisy girl" commercial, which showed a young American girl right before getting hit by a nuclear explosion.

In the days leading up to the election, Johnson led in polls by huge margins against Goldwater.

Because Goldwater was, in principle, against the Civil Rights Act, many Dixiecrats switched from Democrat to Republican to support him.

And here are the results...

Lyndon Johnson easily won, remaining the thirty-sixth President in American history. Actually, he really, *really* dominated. He received 486 electoral votes. Goldwater received just 52 electoral votes.

In terms of the popular vote, this was the most lopsided Presidential election in American history. Johnson got 61.1% of the popular vote. That was also the highest popular vote percentage in American history. Goldwater got just 38.5%.

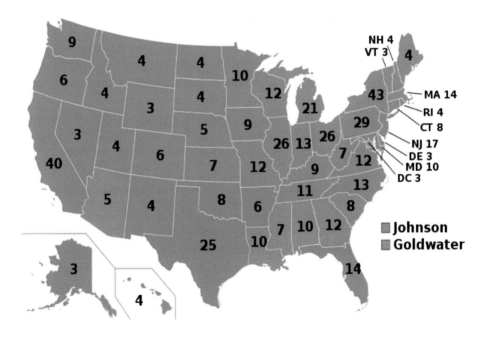

You can probably credit the lopsided victory to the Johnson campaign for successfully making Goldwater look like a dangerous, old fashioned, lunatic. This was about as fear-based as it got for a presidential election. People mostly seemed to vote for Johnson because they were freaked out about Goldwater.

Hubert Humphrey became the thirty-eighth Vice President in American history.

The election of 1964 made clear a new trend that had already been happening for several years- more and more Southerners defined themselves as Republicans instead of Democrats, and this trend only became stronger in the coming years. What led the trend was Democrat support of civil rights legislation, but it really was more than that.

Goldwater's defeat influenced the modern conservative movement, and over the years would lead directly to the election of Ronald Reagan in 1980. Spoiler alert! Oops, I think I was too late with that one.

61.9% of the population voted in this election.

Turn the page for the next election, buddy.

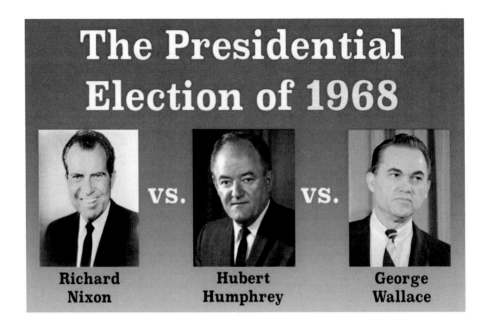

The Presidential Election of 1968

vs. **vs.**

Richard Nixon

Hubert Humphrey

George Wallace

The forty-sixth Presidential election in American history took place on November 5, 1968. Sure, President Lyndon Johnson easily won the 1964 election, but what a difference four years makes. In case you didn't know, the 1960s were probably the most exciting decade of the twentieth century. Society was dramatically changing, and one of the quickest ways to realize this is by comparing music from the beginning of the decade to music from the end of the decade. Not only was there the rise of the hippie counterculture, but there was the rise of the New Left movement and Black Power. 1968 was a crazy year in American history. There were many riots and just a lot of mad people who took to the streets to protest. Martin Luther King, Jr. was assassinated, for crying out loud.

Meanwhile, Johnson's popularity declined dramatically, mostly due to the Vietnam War. Each year during his Presidency, Johnson had sent more and more soldiers to fight in a war that more and more Americans were saying was stupid and pointless. Not only that, the war was not going well at all. It was looking like this might be the first war the United States lost...*ever*. Well, unless you count the Civil War (The War of 1812 was more of a draw).

Despite all this, Johnson decided to run for reelection anyway, but he did have opponents, like Eugene McCarthy, the U.S. Senator from Minnesota, and Robert Kennedy, the brother of John Kennedy and now U.S. Senator from New York. Because the Vietnam War kept getting worse, Johnson didn't do so well with the New Hampshire primary, and he decided to drop out of the race after it.

With Johnson out, Vice President Hubert Humphrey decided to run. In the Democratic primaries, it was basically a three-way race between Humphrey, Kennedy, and McCarthy. Humphrey had supported continuing to send troops to Vietnam, and Kennedy and McCarthy were both strongly anti-war. This would make you think Kennedy and McCarthy were all cozy, and they used to be, but McCarthy was a little annoyed that he was the first one bold enough to challenge Johnson about the war and now Kennedy was wanting all the glory from it. Kennedy and McCarthy debated each other several times, and the two were in a tight race for the most delegates heading into the convention.

But then, there was more tragedy. Robert Kennedy was assassinated in Los Angeles on June 5th by a dude named Sirhan Sirhan, who to this day says he does not remember doing it. Though it was difficult, the Democrats tried to press on after Kennedy's death. Many Kennedy supporters switched to support McCarthy.

However, at the convention, despite violent confrontations between anti-war protesters and the police going on right outside for several days, Hubert Humphrey won the nomination thanks to the party elites backing him. The Democrats went with Edmund Muskie, a U.S. Senator from Maine, as Humphrey's running mate.

The Republicans once again had Richard Nixon, who had returned for another go at it after losing the 1960 election. Nixon was always the frontrunner for the nomination, but George Romney, the Governor of Michigan, posed a big threat early on. Later, Ronald Reagan, the Governor of California, was an even bigger threat. At the convention, a bunch of candidates tried for the nomination, and Republicans also wrote-in a ton of names, like even people from other political parties. This proves there was significant opposition to Nixon, but he won the nomination anyway--barely--and with the help of former Dixiecrat Strom Thurmond, who was now a dedicated Republican thanks to liking Barry Goldwater. The Republicans nominated Spiro Agnew, the Governor of Maryland, as Nixon's running mate.

Well, we haven't heard from third parties in awhile. So it's about time someone like George Wallace came along to challenge the status quo. The newly formed American Independent Party nominated Wallace, the now former Governor of Alabama, for President. Curtis LeMay, the former Chief of Staff of the Air Force, was his running mate. Wallace continued to run on a segregationist platform. However, he was also a populist, appealing to many blue collar workers outside of the South.

Wallace polled as high as 21% in September, but most Americans thought he was just a bit too racist for them. Therefore, as election day drew near, it seemed it would be either Nixon or Humphrey. Nixon, a former Vice President, and Humphrey, the current one. Nixon had a big early lead, but in October Humphrey began to make a comeback in the polls, mostly due to Wallace supporters coming his way.

Nixon campaigned on bringing back "law and order," and promising to end the draft and had a "secret plan" to end the Vietnam War. Humphrey campaigned on continuing and even expanding Johnson's popular Great Society welfare programs. He got a big boost when Johnson announced that the United States would be rolling back its efforts in the war just a few days before the election. On election night, no one seemed to have a clue who would win.

And here are the results...

In another squeaker, this time Richard Nixon came out the winner. He became the thirty-seventh President in American history. The electoral college was deceiving. Nixon received 301 electoral votes and Hubert Humphrey received 191. However, with the popular vote, Nixon got 43.4% and Humphrey got 42.7%. This weird difference between the electoral vote and the popular vote inspired the closest we ever got to ever getting rid of the Electoral College, which was the proposed Bayh-Celler Constitutional amendment, which obviously did not pass.

George Wallace came in third, with 46 electoral votes, which were all in the South, of course. He got 13.5% of the popular vote. Wallace was the last third party presidential candidate to win all of a state's electoral votes.

Spiro Agnew became the thirty-ninth Vice President in American history, and also the one with the best name. Say it aloud. It's fun. Spiro Agnew!

Humphrey should have felt lucky. After 1968, the only way to win the presidential nomination was through the primary process. Humphrey was the last nominee of either major party to win despite not really competing in the primaries.

With this election, the former New Deal coalition, or different groups of people who had all traditionally supported the New Deal programs of FDR, officially fell part. For the rest of the century, the Democrats struggled to get a President elected, unless they were from the South.

60.9% of the population voted in this election.

Turn the page for the next election, buddy.

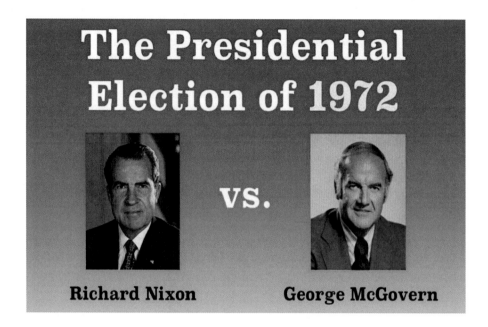

The Presidential Election of 1972

Richard Nixon   vs.   **George McGovern**

The forty-seventh Presidential election in American history took place on November 7, 1972. It was the first one in which Americans aged 18 to 20 could vote, thanks to the recent passage of the 26th Amendment to the Constitution.

Richard Nixon acted like a madman. Well, he pretended to, making the Soviet Union and North Vietnam think he was unpredictable and crazy so that they would be more afraid of the United States. Really though, Nixon just wanted the Vietnam War over, but he found it difficult to just bring all the troops home at once. In some ways, he made the conflict worse after he continued to bomb Cambodia. Still, each year, more and more American troops came back home.

Nixon seemed to contradict himself with foreign policy. On one hand, he wanted more involvement abroad to prevent the spread of Communism, including having the C.I.A. continue to secretly take out Communist leaders in foreign countries. On the other hand, Nixon advocated a policy called detente, which is a fancy word for easing relations between two countries. Nixon visited Communist China, for example, which was an important step in improving relations with them.

Going into the election, Nixon had an approval rating of over 60%, but he did have two opponents trying to prevent him getting renominated by the Republicans. Pete McCloskey, a U.S. Representative from California, ran against him because he thought all the troops from Vietnam should have been brought home a long time ago. Nixon's other opponent was John Ashbrook, a U.S. Representative from Ohio, who criticized Nixon for being too liberal and too much of a big government-guy. Ashbrook was also against detente.

But McCloskey and Ashbrook never had much of a chance. Nixon was easily renominated, with Vice President Spiro Agnew again as his running mate.

Fifteen people declared themselves as candidates for the Democratic Party. One of them, Shirley Chisholm, a U.S. Representative from New York, became the first African American to run for a major party nomination. Another notable female candidate was Patsy Mink, a U.S. Representative from Hawaii.

The guy who was the favorite for the nomination originally was Senate Majority Whip Ted Kennedy, the youngest brother of John and Robert Kennedy. But he said he wouldn't be a candidate. Perhaps he was afraid he would be assassinated?

Hubert Humphrey went ahead and gave it another go, but did not campaign aggressively. It's almost like he didn't want to go through it all again. Edmund Muskie, Humphrey's running mate in 1968, was the frontrunner for awhile until a successful smear campaign shook him up, to a point where it looked like he was crying, and there's no crying in baseball, I mean politics, even if they were just snowflakes, and this hurt his chances, believe it or not.

Then there was George Wallace, who was back with the Democratic Party after leaving them in 1968 with his fairly successful third party run. Wallace, surprisingly, did well in the primaries again, but his campaign was cut short after he was shot multiple times by a kid named Arthur Bremer, who, believe it or not, was released from prison back in 2007 for good behavior and is still alive. Wallace survived, but he was paralyzed from the waist down and would be in tremendous pain for the rest of his life.

So that just leaves George McGovern, a U.S. Senator from South Dakota who had a big grassroots campaign. McGovern stood out as the leading anti-war candidate, who also thought all the troops from Vietnam should have been brought home a long time ago. Although the Democratic Party establishment again wanted Hubert Humphrey as their guy, the grassroots movement to get McGovern as the nominee overcame them. McGovern became the nominee, and, what became known as the McGovern Commission, or the principle that the most *primary votes* should actually determine who the nominee was, has been the norm ever since. Some of the Democratic Party establishment didn't like McGovern, though, and refused to support him.

The Democrats nominated Thomas Eagleton, a U.S. Senator from Missouri, as his running mate. As it turns out, Eagleton had health concerns since it was revealed he had previously been treated for depression with electroshock therapy, and was pressured to drop out of the race. After Eagleton dropped out, McGovern had a hard time finding his replacement. He asked six different people to be his running mate, and they all turned him down. That's a little embarrassing. Finally, Sargent Shriver, a brother-in-law to the Kennedys and a former Ambassador to France, became his running mate.

The American Independent Party, which nominated George Wallace in 1968, this time nominated John Schmitz, an extremely conservative U.S. Representative from California, for President, and Thomas Anderson, a writer and farmer originally from Tennessee, for Vice President.

But it appeared to be another classic two-way race, between Nixon and McGovern. Just like Goldwater in 1964, this time McGovern was successfully portrayed as a "radical." Opponents said his foreign policy and views on the Vietnam War were unrealistic and that he leaned too far to the left. He did, after all, call for a guaranteed minimum income for the poor, but today is known as universal basic income.

Heading into the election, it just wasn't looking so good for McGovern.

And here are the results...

Richard Nixon easily won reelection, receiving 520 electoral votes. He got 60.7% of the popular vote. By all accounts, Nixon destroyed McGovern. McGovern received only 17 electoral votes, which was just Massachusetts and the District of Columbia. He got just 37.5% of the popular vote. Nixon received nearly 18 million more votes than McGovern, the widest margin of any presidential election in American history. This was the first election in which California had the most electoral votes, and it has been that way ever since.

John Schmitz came in third with 1.4% of the popular vote.

You may also notice something else weird about the electoral map. In Virginia, one faithless elector who said he'd vote for Nixon instead voted for the Libertarian Party candidate, John Hospers. This was the first election in which the Libertarian Party participated.

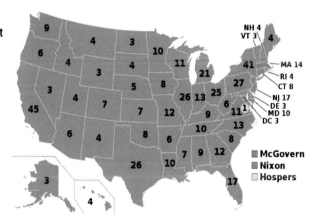

55.2% of the population voted in this election.

Turn the page for the next election, buddy.

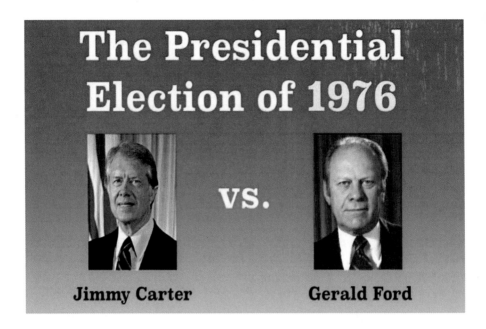

The Presidential Election of 1976

Jimmy Carter vs. **Gerald Ford**

The forty-eighth Presidential election in American history took place on November 2, 1976. The country was now over 200 years old, but during this time an increasing number of Americans didn't seem to trust their government. Richard Nixon might be the reason why. Remember how he won big in the 1972 election? Well, as it turns out, his campaign that year was up to some shady stuff. Some of his supporters broke into the Democratic National Committee headquarters at the Watergate office complex in Washington, D.C. in order to spy on them. They were busted, and this was eventually known as the Watergate scandal.

As it turns out, the Nixon administration was involved and later tried to cover it up. Nixon was forced to give up audio recordings that proved this. Facing impeachment by the House of Representatives and likely getting fired by the Senate, Nixon resigned on August 9, 1974. Just like that, he was gone.

Gerald Ford, the Vice President, was sworn in as the thirty-eighth President in American history. Hold up! What happened to Spiro Agnew? Spiro Agnew had actually resigned the year before. He had his own scandal involving him receiving illegal bribes back when he was the Governor of Maryland, and then he got in trouble for tax evasion. So Nixon nominated Ford, a dude from Michigan who at the time was the House Minority Leader. Congress overwhelmingly approved the nomination. Good thing the fairly recently passed 25th Amendment to the Constitution said they could now do this.

Also because of the 25th Amendment, Nelson Rockefeller became the forty-first Vice President in American history.

So what is one of the first things that Gerald Ford does? Well, he pardons Richard Nixon. All, that's so sweet of him.

Ford was President during a tricky time- the Vietnam War was ending as the Americans left and let South Vietnam fall, which was a humbling defeat, and the economy wasn't doing so well back at home. The U.S. dealt with stagflation, which is when things basically cost a lot while unemployment goes up and companies produce less.

In 1976, Ford tried to get the Republican nomination for President as the only sitting President who had never been elected to national office, and he had an impressive challenger. Ronald Reagan, the now former governor of California, nearly took the nomination. Going into the Republican Convention, the two were dead even. However, Ford won the nomination narrowly on the first ballot. The Republicans nominated Bob Dole, a U.S. Senator from my home state of Kansas, as his running mate.

Just like in 1972, many sought the Democratic Party nomination. Four stood out in the beginning. Henry Jackson, a U.S. Senator from Washington, Mo Udall, a U.S. Representative from Arizona, Jerry Brown, the Governor of California and son of former California Governor Pat Brown, and George Wallace, who, despite being shot and paralyzed during the last election effort, was still going strong. Well none of those four saw Jimmy Carter coming.
Carter, a former Governor of Georgia, took everyone by surprise by winning the early Iowa caucus and New Hampshire primary. Henry Jackson didn't even compete in those, and boy was that a big mistake- he never recovered. Ever since then, the media has spent extra special attention to Iowa and New Hampshire, you may have noticed.

Anyway, Carter capitalized on the fact that he was a DC outsider and a centrist from the South to become a successful dark horse candidate. Despite an ABC movement, or Anybody But Carter movement, Carter got the nomination at the convention, with Walter Mondale, a U.S. Senator from Minnesota, as his running mate.

One third party candidate I will mention was Eugene McCarthy, our boy from the 1968 election, who had since split from the Democratic Party and now ran as an independent candidate.

But the Democrats and Republicans had the money. Carter generally led in the polls over Ford, and Ford said stupid things like "there is no Soviet domination of Eastern Europe and there never will be under a Ford administration." But then again, Carter was talking about lusting for women other than his wife to *Playboy Magazine*, so the race appeared to remain close.

Bob Dole and Walter Mondale participated in the first-ever formal vice presidential candidate debate. During the debate, Dole talked trash about all the Democratic presidents of the 20th century, saying their military unpreparedness led to all the wars fought in the century. This actually backfired and some argue hurt the Republican ticket.

And here are the results...

Jimmy Carter won, becoming the thirty-ninth President in American history. He received 297 electoral votes. Gerald Ford received 240. Ford actually won 27 states and Carter just 23, and this was the closest electoral vote result since the election of 1916. One faithless elector in Washington State actually gave their electoral vote to Ronald Reagan.

The popular vote was fairly close, too. Carter got 50.1%, while Ford got 48%. Maybe because he was a Southern dude, Carter did well in the South. In fact, Carter was the first Democrat since John F. Kennedy to carry states in the Deep South.

Walter Mondale became the forty-second Vice President in American history.

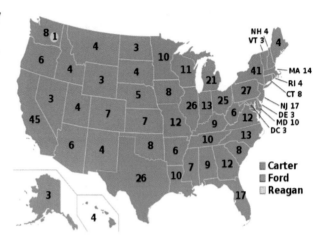

This election is weird because all four of the major party presidential and vice presidential candidates at some point in their lives were losers. Well, they were losers of a presidential election race, that is.

53.6% of the population voted in this election.

Turn the page for the next election, buddy.

The Presidential Election of 1980

Ronald Reagan vs. **Jimmy Carter** vs. **John Anderson**

The forty-ninth Presidential election in American history took place on November 4, 1980. As President, Jimmy Carter faced quite a few obstacles, and things just weren't all peachy. The country faced low economic growth, high inflation and interest rates, and an energy crisis, in which the prices of oil went way up since supply went down in certain areas. This shortage was partially caused by the Iranian Revolution of 1979, in which a new Islamic government hostile to the United States overthrew the old one.

And this soon led to the Iranian Hostage Crisis, in which 52 American diplomats and citizens were held hostage after a group of Iranian revolutionaries took over the U.S. Embassy in Tehran. Carter tried applying economic and diplomatic pressure on the Iranians to get the hostages released, but ultimately, by the time the election rolled around, he was unsuccessful in getting them freed.

As Carter sought renomination by the Democratic Party, he did face challengers. His leading opponent was Ted Kennedy. This was the toughest primary race a sitting President had to go through to seek his party's renomination since President Taft sought renomination in the election of 1912, which as you already know ended up splitting the Republican Party. Carter and Kennedy were in a tight race, and some people tried to get Edmund Muskie, who was now the Secretary of State, to run against them, just to break apart the deadlock between the two. It didn't work, but Carter had more delegates than Kennedy going into the convention, and he won renomination, with Walter Mondale also renominated for Vice President.

Ronald Reagan was easily the favorite to win the Republican nomination, but he did have several opponents. The biggest one was George Herbert Walker Bush, the former CIA director and U.S. Representative from Texas, but there was also John B. Anderson, a U.S. Representative from Illinois. Anderson stood out among the crowd of Republicans because of a great debate performance against his other Republican challengers. He eloquently expressed himself and said things none of the other candidates dared say, like saying that lowering taxes, increasing defense spending, and balancing the budget could not all happen at the same time. After this, Anderson got a lot of media attention.

Still, no one could take on the popular Ronald Reagan, who it seems had been preparing for this moment for a very long time. Reagan got the nomination, with Bush as his running mate.

Meanwhile, Anderson had decided to leave the Republican Party and run as an independent candidate, mostly as a centrist, or as the moderate guy who argued that Reagan was much too conservative and Carter much too liberal. Patrick Lucey, a former Democratic governor of Wisconsin and Ambassador to Mexico in the Carter administration, was Anderson's running mate.

The Libertarian Party by this time had started to gain some momentum. They nominated Ed Clark, a lawyer who had previously ran for governor of California as the third party candidate but lost. David Koch, a businessman and engineer from Kansas, was his running mate. Koch later became famous, or infamous, depending on who you ask, for his association with his brother, Charles, and influencing elections. Koch pledged part of his personal fortune to the campaign.

The two front runners, Reagan and Carter, were neck and neck. Reagan ran a campaign of optimism, while Carter's campaign seemed to be more negative, attacking Reagan for being too far to the right. Reagan called for more military spending, while at the same time calling for a smaller government. Wait, what? Carter's campaign had to defend the Iranian hostage crisis, support for the Equal Rights Amendment to the constitution, which was supposed to guarantee equality for women but by 1980 was not as popular, and a struggling economy.

Not only that, but when the League of Women Voters invited Carter to debate both Reagan and Anderson, Carter turned it down because Anderson was invited. So the debate was a bit weird, with just Reagan and Anderson going at it. Anderson was polling at around 20 percent at the time. After the debate, Anderson's poll numbers dropped, and the League asked Carter again to join just Reagan this time for a debate one week before the election. Carter accepted. The debate had really high ratings, and by most accounts Reagan dominated, even though his campaign may have had access to Carter's notes preparing for the debate ahead of time.

And here are the results...

Ronald Reagan easily won, becoming the fortieth President in American history. He received 489 electoral votes, the most ever for a President elected for the first time. It was pretty impressive for a guy who was called a radical by opponents for so long. He also got a strong 50.7% of the popular vote. He was the oldest President ever elected up to that point in American history.

Jimmy Carter received just 49 electoral votes and 41% of the popular vote. In terms of the popular vote, this was the worst performance by an incumbent President in an election since Herbert Hoover in the election of 1932. In terms of the electoral vote, this was the most lopsided defeat for any incumbent president in an election where only two candidates received electoral votes.

In third place, John Anderson, who didn't get electoral votes but received a respectable 6.6% of the popular vote. Anderson promptly faded into obscurity after this election.

Ed Clark finished fourth with 1.1%, the best showing for the Libertarian Party up to that point.

George H.W. Bush became the forty-third Vice President in American history.

Reagan was so popular that he helped the Republicans regain control of the Senate for the first time since 1952. This election marked the beginning of what became known as the Reagan Revolution, which marked a dramatic conservative shift in national politics. Within minutes after Reagan was sworn into office, the Iranian hostages were formally released, and of course Reagan got all the credit, even though the Carter administration did all the work before that.

52.6% of the population voted in this election.

Turn the page for the next election, buddy.

The Presidential Election of 1984

VS.

Ronald Reagan   **Walter Mondale**

The fiftieth Presidential election in American history took place on November 6, 1984, on my third birthday. Yep, this was the first presidential election I was alive to witness, although I don't remember it at all.

Anyway, Ronald Reagan was easily renominated as the Republican nominee after a strong first term. The economy had rebounded, and many Americans seemed to credit Reagan for getting the rest of the world to respect the country more. Sure, the government didn't shrink much, and military spending went way up, but that seemed to be what everyone wanted. Reagan talked trash about the Soviet Union, but more discreetly took the beginning steps to help end the Cold War.

Vice President George H.W. Bush was also easily renominated. This was the only time both a vice presidential roll call and presidential roll call was done at the same time.

While at least eight Democrats sought their party's nomination, only three won any state primaries. One was Jesse Jackson, a civil rights activist and Baptist minister, and the first African American to be a serious contender for the Presidency. Another was Gary Hart, a U.S. Senator from Colorado, who became the main rival to Walter Mondale, the former Vice President in the Carter administration, who appeared to be the favorite. While Hart came close, but Mondale came out as the winner. In a somewhat surprising move, Mondale went with Geraldine Ferraro, a U.S. Representative from New York, as his running mate. She became the first major party female vice presidential candidate in American history. Mondale and the Democrats probably figured, what the heck, Reagan is so popular, we need to do whatever we possibly can to get the attention of voters to sway them our way.

Despite his old age—Reagan was now 73—he seemed unstoppable. Still, opponents questioned how well he could continue to be the commander in chief at his age. In response, at one of the debates between him and Mondale, he joked, "I will not make age an issue of this campaign. I am not going to exploit, for political purposes, my opponent's youth and inexperience."

Mondale criticized Reagan's supply side economics, which is often called "trickle-down economics," and called attention to the rising budget deficits. His solution? Raise taxes. Sure, the people love hearing that. Despite Ferraro being the first major party female vice presidential candidate, she didn't generate the excitement that Democrats had originally anticipated.

And here are the results...

Oh my goodness. It was a blowout. Reagan destroyed Mondale, easily winning reelection. He received 525 electoral votes. That was every state except for Mondale's home state of Minnesota and the District of Columbia. So yeah, Mondale just received 13 electoral votes.

Reagan's 525 electoral votes are the most ever received by a presidential candidate.

The popular vote wasn't quite as lopsided. Thanks Electoral College for deceiving us yet again! Reagan got 58.8%, which was still incredibly high, and Mondale got just 40.6%. I guess that still was lopsided. We now

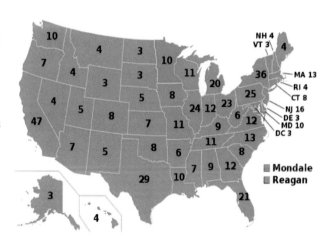

know that millions of Democrats even voted for Reagan. Anyway, Reagan officially became the oldest candidate to ever win a presidential election.

The next month, a White House social aide asked Reagan what he wanted for Christmas. Reagan jokingly replied, "Well, Minnesota would have been nice."

53.3% of the population voted in this election.

Turn the page for the next election, buddy.

The Presidential Election of 1988

George H.W. Bush   VS.   **Michael Dukakis**

The fifty-first Presidential election in American history took place on November 8, 1988. It was the earliest one I actually remembered. By many accounts, Ronald Reagan had a solid Presidency. He helped end the Cold War, and the economy remained strong. However, there was some bad stuff, too. For example, there was the Iran Contra Affair, in which the Reagan administration secretly sold weapons to Iran in exchange for hostages, but also to pay the Contras, a rebel group in Nicaragua. Oh yeah, and it was later revealed the C.I.A. was also sneaking in and selling millions of dollars worth of cocaine and sending the profits it made also to the Contras.

But most Americans didn't know about that, and when Reagan pointed to George H.W. Bush, his Vice President, as the best man to be his successor, many Republicans were on board. Bush did face some challengers, though. One who stood out was Bob Dole, the U.S. Senator from Kansas who was Gerald Ford's running mate back when they failed to win the election of 1976. Another was, believe it or not, Pat Robertson, the former Southern Baptist minister and media mogul. In the Iowa caucus, Bush came in third, behind both Dole and Robertson. But Bush rebounded, eventually taking a strong lead to easily win the Republican nomination, with Dan Quayle, a young U.S. Senator from Indiana, as his running mate. Quayle was a controversial pick among Republicans, though, because he was criticized for his lack of experience and sometimes stumbled over his words.

The Democrats had the Seven Dwarfs. No, not the Seven Dwarfs you're probably thinking about from the Snow White story. The Seven Dwarfs of the 1988 presidential election were what critics called the seven leading contenders for the Democratic nomination. They included

Jesse Jackson, who was back for a second try, Al Gore, another young U.S. Senator from Tennessee, Bruce Babbitt, the Governor of Arizona, Joe Biden, a U.S. Senator from Delaware. Then there was Richard Gephardt, a U.S. Representative from Missouri. There was the great songwriter Paul Simon. Oops. No, not *that* Paul Simon. I'm talking about the one who was a U.S. Senator from Illinois, who looked very good in bow ties. Finally, there was Michael Dukakis, the Governor of Massachusetts.

Now, the Democrats tried to recruit New York Governor Mario Cuomo to run, but he declined. Then there was Gary Hart, who at first seemed destined to become the nominee and the party's leader of the future. However, the media all of sudden decided to pry into his personal life, and, as it turns out, he was cheating on his wife. Many of his supporters turned against him after they found this out, and he ended up suspending his campaign because of it. Wow, times have changed.

With no clear frontrunner, the Democrats had a long and exciting primary race. In the end, it was Governor Dukakis who got the nomination. Jesse Jackson finished second, and his supporters argued he should be Dukakis' running mate, but Dukakis disagreed, instead choosing Lloyd Bentsen, a U.S. Senator from Texas.

The Bush campaign aggressively attacked Dukakis. Bush capitalized on the word "liberal," which was now considered by many a dirty word to call a politician. He called Dukakis a liberal when it came to everything. A guy named Lee Atwater helped circulate rumours to the media that Dukakis's wife Kitty had burned an American flag to protest the Vietnam War, even though it wasn't true. Bush argued Dukakis was ignorant when it came to the military.

And Dukakis responded poorly to these criticisms and rumours. I mean, he staged a photo op where he rode around in a tank to try to prove he knew military matters, and it backfired horribly. That, a poor debate performance, and the fact that Bush was capitalizing on a good economy and Reagan's popularity all greatly hurt Dukakis.

And here are the results...

George Herbert Walker Bush easily won, becoming the forty-first President in American history. He received 426 electoral votes and 53.4% of the popular vote. Surprisingly, since this election, no candidate has been able to match or surpass these numbers.

Michael Dukakis received just 111 electoral votes and 45.6% of the popular vote.

Margaret Leach, a member of the West Virginia House of Delegates, was an elector and had pledged her vote to Dukakis. However, she instead cast her vote to Bentsen to protest the Electoral College's winner-take-all system.

Bush became the first sitting Vice President to win a presidential election in 152 years- the last one was Martin Van Buren back in 1836.

Dan Quayle became the forty-fourth Vice President in American history.

Bush had campaigned as the candidate who promised to never ever raise taxes. We'll see if that holds up.

50.2% of the population voted in this election.

Turn the page for the next election, buddy.

The Presidential Election of 1992

Bill Clinton vs. **George H.W. Bush** vs. **Ross Perot**

The fifty-second Presidential election in American history took place on November 3, 1992. George H.W. Bush had alienated most conservatives by straight up breaking that pledge to not raise taxes. I mean, *he tried*, but he ended up having to give in and compromise with the Democrat-controlled Congress. Plus, the economy went back into a recession.

And yet, Bush remained popular with the majority of Americans. After the United States and coalition forces kicked butt in the Persian Gulf War, his approval rating got as high as 89%. This likely helped Bush get the Republican renomination, with Vice President Dan Quayle again as his running mate. However, it's worth noting that Pat Buchanan, a journalist and former advisor to Presidents Richard Nixon, Gerald Ford, and Ronald Reagan, challenged Bush and put up a good fight. Buchanan's main beef with Bush was the fact that he raised taxes.

The Democratic Party again had several candidates interested in their nomination. U.S. Senator Al Gore would have run again, but his son was recovering from a horrible car accident, so he decided not to. One of the candidates who ran was Bob Kerrey, a U.S. Senator from Nebraska, who I am only mentioning because I had a fantastic conversation with him when I used to live in Omaha, but yeah...he couldn't get any momentum. The leading three contenders were Bill Clinton, the Governor of Arkansas, Jerry Brown, the former Governor of California, and Paul Tsongas, a former U.S. Senator from Massachusetts.

Despite the fact that several scandals seemed to follow Bill Clinton no matter where he went, including a scandal that alleged he cheated on his wife, Hillary Clinton, his charm won over most Democrats. Clinton became the nominee, and he asked Al Gore to be his running mate.

Back in February of 1992, a billionaire businessman named Ross Perot appeared on Larry King Live to open the possibility of running for President, despite the fact that he had never held public office before. Soon after, a huge grassroots movement swept the country to get Perot on the ballot in every state. Getting on the ballot in every state was a big deal back then for a third party candidate, and it still is. James Stockdale, a war hero and former prisoner of war in Vietnam, was Perot's running mate.

By May, believe it or not, he was the frontrunner, leading over both Bush and Clinton in the polls. However, by July the establishment media had been regularly attacking him, and he didn't know how to handle it well. He was, after all, getting attacked by both Republicans and Democrats. There were also internal issues within his campaign. And then, in July, almost seemingly out of the blue, Perot dropped out of the race. To this day, it remains a mystery why he exactly did this. He later explained it was to protect his daughter, but that still seems like a weird excuse. His supporters felt betrayed.

Flash forward to October, and all of sudden Perot said he was back in the race. He qualified for the presidential debates, and it was only the second time a third party candidate was allowed in a general election televised debate- the first being John Anderson back in 1980. However, these debates were extra special because it was the only time in American history where three candidates all got to debate each other at the same time on TV. And the debates were exciting!

This was a classic three-way race. It really was. Supporters of all three candidates thought their candidate had a good chance to win up until the end. Clinton and Perot attacked Bush because of the lagging economy. Clinton remained a charmer, but critics pointed out character flaws. In addition to allegations of cheating on his wife, Clinton was criticized for dodging the draft during the Vietnam War and smoking marijuana. Oh, how the times have changed.

Ross Perot, despite being a billionaire who spent tens of millions of dollars of his own money to run his campaign, ran as the outsider who wanted to end crony capitalism and the special interests in Washington. Perot stood out as the only candidate who criticized the controversial NAFTA, or North American Free Trade Agreement. He could never regain the momentum he had back in the spring, however, distantly in third place behind Bush and Clinton in the polls right before election day.

And here are the results...

Bill Clinton won, becoming the forty-second President in American history. He received 370 electoral votes and 43% of the popular vote. George H.W. Bush finished second, receiving 168 electoral votes and 37.5% of the popular vote. Ross Perot finished third, receiving 18.9% of the popular vote but no electoral votes as his support was pretty consistent across the country. It was the best third party performance in the popular vote since the presidential election of 1912.

Al Gore became the forty-fifth Vice President in American history.

Clinton was the first Democrat since Jimmy Carter to become President. He united Democrats across the country with his centrist, or "Third Way" views. Clinton became the poster boy for a new group of Democrats that became known as the New Democrats, who appealed a lot to people who had moderate views.

Republicans blamed Perot for being a "spoiler," but there is no evidence that backs this up. Perot did influence the race, however, as Clinton made it a priority to balance the budget after he became President.

Really, the Republicans should have blamed Bush for losing this election. He had the lowest percentage total for a sitting President seeking reelection since William Howard Taft, also in the election of 1912. He also had the lowest percentage for a major-party candidate since Alf Landon in the election of 1936.

55.2% of the population voted in this election.

Turn the page for the next election, buddy.

The Presidential Election of 1996

Bill Clinton vs. **Bob Dole** vs. **Ross Perot**

The fifty-third Presidential election in American history took place on November 5, 1996. It featured a dude from Kansas, a dude from Arkansas, and another dude from Texas.

At first, it wasn't looking so good for Bill Clinton. He faced the Republican Revolution of 1994, in which the Republican Party regained control of both houses of Congress and state governments after a long hiatus. In fact, this was the first time Republicans held the majority in the House of Representatives in 40 years. Clinton also hadn't held up to promises to cut taxes and reduce the deficit. Plus, he wanted to take away the Second Amendment. Oh I joke! But seriously, he signed the Federal Assault Weapons Ban, which didn't get him many friends with the National Rifle Association.

However, the economy was getting better, and the United States was the only superpower left on the world stage, so Americans were like, "What's up, now, world?" Clinton maybe had a chance. He and Vice President Al Gore were easily renominated.

Many Republicans fought for the nomination, but the top three contenders were Steve Forbes, a publishing executive from New Jersey, Pat Buchanan, who still had strong support despite his losing effort in 1992, and Bob Dole, the U.S. Senator from Kansas who ran back in 1988. Steve Forbes stood out as a dude who really pushed for a flat income tax. Pat Buchanan was the paleoconservative type, kind of like Alex Jones but not nearly as crazy. Dole, who was more moderate and more of an establishment type, of course won the nomination, with Buchanan coming in second and Steve Forbes coming in third. Dole picked Jack Kemp, a former U.S. Representative from New York, former Secretary of Housing and Urban Development, and former professional football player, as his running mate.

Also, Texas billionaire Ross Perot was back. He and his supporters created a new political party called the Reform Party. Perot originally did not want to run again, but after the Federal Election Commission said that the Reform Party would only get federal matching funds if Perot ran, Perot changed his mind and entered the race. However, the Commission on Presidential Debates, made up of only Democrats and Republicans by the way, arbitrarily changed its rules for the 1996 debates to not include Perot. Many argue that his poll numbers were hurt because he wasn't invited to the debates. Perot's running mate was Pat Choate, an economist from Texas.

However, Bill Clinton and Bob Dole were allowed to debate. Age seemed to be an issue with the campaigns. Dole, who was 73 years old, had to fight off the perception that he was an old fogey and out of touch with the issues. He mistakenly referred to the Los Angeles Dodgers as the "Brooklyn Dodgers," even though the Dodgers had left Brooklyn 38 years earlier. At a stop in California, he fell off a stage. However, to show everyone he was healthy, Dole released his medical records, and he even joked that the reason why he fell was that he was just trying to do the Macarena. Dole tried to use his age to his advantage, arguing that he came from the great generation that won World War 2, while his opponent, Clinton, was just a spoiled Baby Boomer.

While Clinton didn't directly attack Dole about his age, Clinton did question the age of Dole's ideas. Oh snap!

And here are the results...

Bill Clinton easily won reelection, receiving 379 electoral votes and 49.2% of the popular vote. He was the first Democrat to win reelection since Franklin Roosevelt. Also, at 50 years and 2 months old, he became the youngest President to ever be reelected.

Bob Dole received 159 electoral votes and 40.7% of the popular vote. That old fogey Bob Dole, by the way, is still alive and still active, 24 years later. I spent many months in a building named after him and dedicated to him learning how to produce awesome videos at the University of Kansas, which was where he went to school, too.

Ross Perot finished third, again not receiving any electoral votes and getting much less of the popular vote than he did in 1992. Still, he got a respectable 8.4% of the popular vote. This was the last time a third party candidate got more than 4% of the vote. After this election, a lawsuit was filed on Perot's behalf against the Commission on Presidential Debates.

Despite Dole losing, the Republican Party still kept its majority in Congress.

49% of the population voted in this election.

Turn the page for the next election, buddy.

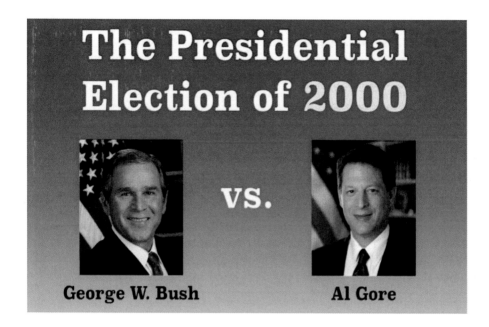

The Presidential Election of 2000

VS.

George W. Bush

Al Gore

The fifty-fourth Presidential election in American history took place on November 7, 2000. It was the first election I could finally vote in! And wow, was it a messed up one. We wouldn't even know who won until over a month later.

As Bill Clinton left office, the economy was strong, and he had a fairly high approval rating. Sure, there was the whole impeachment thing due to lying under oath about an affair with his intern, Monica Lewinsky. Oh yeah, and there was Vince Foster's suicide, Whitewater, Travelgate, Filegate, and so forth and so on, but many argue the United States was preparing to enter the twenty-first century stronger than ever before. Because of this, the Democratic Party went with Clinton's Vice President, Al Gore, to be their nominee for President. His only real opponent trying to get the nomination was Bill Bradley, the former U.S. Senator from New Jersey and former professional basketball player. But Bradley withdrew in March, so it was Gore, with Joe Lieberman, a U.S. Senator from Connecticut, as his running mate. Lieberman was the first practicing Jewish candidate on a major political party presidential ticket.

The Republican Party originally had many candidates trying for the nomination, but most of them didn't stand much of a chance against George W. Bush, the popular Governor of Texas and son of George H.W. Bush. Bush's main opponent in the primaries was John McCain, a U.S. Senator from Arizona and war hero who was tortured as a POW in the Vietnam War. However, after a poor showing on Super Tuesday, the day when there are a bunch of primary elections at once across the country, McCain dropped out. One guy who stuck around until right before the convention was Alan Keyes, a former diplomat in the Reagan administration. He just kept fighting. Also, one thing that is absolutely true, that I actually quite admire, is that Alan Keyes was the first presidential candidate in American history to ever jump into a mosh pit on the campaign trail. Michael Moore jokingly gave him his endorsement after he featured the historic moment on his show *The Awful Truth*.

Anyway, yeah George W. Bush won. You know that, don't you? He had all the right friends in the right places, the right last name, and oh yeah, a lot of people loved him. Bush asked Dick Cheney, a former Secretary of Defense, to lead a team to help him find a running mate, but in the end, Bush just went with Cheney to be his running mate, which was maybe Cheney's plan all along. However, because Cheney also lived in Texas, he had to change his voting registration back to his old home of Wyoming, because otherwise the electoral votes they would presumably get from Texas would not count.

While there were a lot of third party candidates, I will only mention the Green Party for this election. The Green Party had been around in some form or another since the 1980s, and had a platform that focused on environmental causes. They nominated Ralph Nader, the famous activist and lawyer who had sparked reform by getting numerous consumer protection laws passed. The Green Party also nominated Winona LaDuke, an activist, economist, and writer from California, as Nader's running mate. Both Nader and LaDuke had run together back in 1996, but had gotten less than 1% of the vote, which is why I didn't even mention them in that episode.

The two frontrunners, Bush and Gore, mostly focused on domestic issues. Bill Clinton's impeachment and the associated scandal with Monica Lewinsky did cast a shadow on the campaign, but Gore tried to convince Americans he was not Clinton. He rarely appeared with Clinton on the campaign trail, and some say this actually hurt his campaign. Bush called for a more humble foreign policy and more unity and less partisanship in Washington. Nader, meanwhile, had exciting rallies in places like Madison Square Garden.

And here are the results....

Al Gore won, becoming our- wait a minute. Ok, please stand by. Apparently in Florida it was too close to call. At first, it appeared that Gore had won the state, which meant that he would have won the election. However, then some news organizations began calling the state for Bush.

Who won?

The next day, November 8th, the final votes were finally counted. Bush had a slight lead, but the lead was so small that Florida law required a mandatory recount. After the recount later that week, Bush's lead had shrunk to just 300 votes. Then, after counting overseas military ballots, Bush's lead went up to 930 votes. Gore wanted more manual recounts, and the Florida Supreme Court extended the deadline to November 26th. By this time, Bush and Gore were fighting each other in court. Out on the streets, people were protesting on both sides. It got pretty heated.

Photo credit: Elvert Barnes

Ultimately, the United States Supreme Court stepped in and stopped the recount with a vote of 7-2 and 5-4. They argued that the Florida Supreme Court's plan for recounting ballots, using different vote-counting standards from county to county and poor oversight over the entire process, was unconstitutional.

Therefore, the results stood. At the time, the certified count had Bush ahead in Florida by 537 votes. So, George W. Bush became the forty-third President in American history, more than a month after Election Day. He received 271 electoral votes. Al Gore ended up with 266 electoral votes. What was frustrating for Gore voters was that Al Gore actually won the popular vote. He got 48.4% and Bush got 47.9%. Gore received 543,895 more votes than Bush, but still lost the election. This was the fourth of five times in American history in which the winner lost the popular vote but won the presidency. Again, a growing number of Americans protested the Electoral College.

Ralph Nader finished third with no electoral votes but 2.7% of the popular vote. Almost immediately, Al Gore supporters blamed Nader for spoiling the election, but there is little evidence to support this was true.

Dick Cheney became the forty-sixth Vice President in American history.

It was one of the closest elections in American history. Since then, many studies have examined the ballots to see if the result would have been different if there was another recount- but there is no definitive answer, so that's pretty much why people still argue

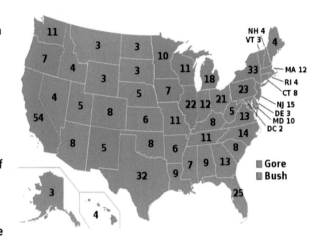

about the election to this day, especially when you look at the dramatic events that unfolded during Bush's first term in office.

51.2% of the population voted in this election.

Turn the page for the next election, buddy.

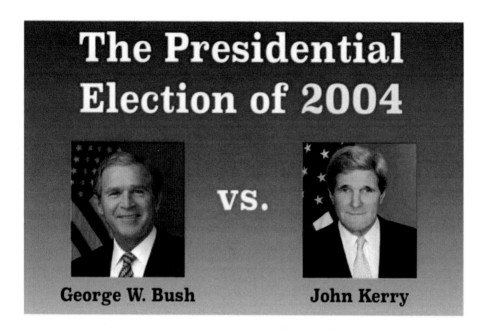

The Presidential Election of 2004

George W. Bush   vs.   **John Kerry**

The fifty-fifth Presidential election in American history took place on November 2, 2004. A lot had changed since the last election. Just eight months after George W. Bush became President, terrorists attacked the United States. On September 11, 2001, they hijacked four planes, crashing two of them into the Twin Towers of the World Trade Center and another into the Pentagon building. Passengers of the fourth plane regained control to prevent it from hitting its target, which was likely the White House or the Capitol Building in Washington, DC. However, that plane crashed in rural Pennsylvania, killing everyone on board. In total, the attack killed almost 3,000 people and the terrorists got exactly what they wanted- Americans were scared.

In response, George W. Bush took swift action declaring a War on Terrorism. Congress passed the Authorization for Use of Military Force Against Terrorists, which pretty much gave Bush lots of leeway in going after those responsible for what became known as the 9/11 attacks.

Bush's main objective was to destroy Al Qaeda, the terrorist group who took responsibility for 9/11. Many believed that the Taliban, the Afghanistan government at the time, was providing a safe haven for Al Qaeda. Bush demanded the Taliban turn over Osama bin Laden and other al-Qaeda leaders hiding out there or face attack. The Taliban didn't cooperate, so Bush sent troops to invade Afghanistan and overthrow their government. Even today, 19 years later, the United States is still dropping bombs on targets in Afghanistan.

The War on Terrorism only got bigger. In 2003, Bush sent troops to Iraq to take over and overthrow their dictator Saddam Hussein. So what did Iraq have to do with 9/11? Well, not much, but the Bush administration claimed that Hussein was working with Al Qaeda and that they had weapons of mass destruction. However, as it turns out, this was not true at all. The decision to invade Iraq was controversial, with protests in the street similar to the protests against the Vietnam War decades before. The initial overthrow wasn't as controversial, but after Bush declared "mission accomplished," basically saying the war was over, American troops stayed there to nation build. This also proved to be controversial, because as the United States tried to rebuild Iraq and have them establish a new government similar to theirs, it just wasn't going so well.

As Bush and Vice President Dick Cheney both sought reelection, there was no end to the Iraq War in sight. Still, they remained popular within the Republican Party, especially after capturing Saddam Hussein, and were both easily renominated.

Many candidates fought for the Democratic Party presidential nomination, but really just three stood out as serious contenders. One was John Edwards, a U.S. Senator from North Carolina. Another was Howard Dean, the former governor of Vermont. Dean was the first candidate to really use the internet to his campaign's advantage. His support was very grassroots, and he had passionate followers. Dean stood out among the crowd because he was one of the few Democrats to actively speak out against the Iraq War. However, the media kept playing a bizarre scream he made at a rally. Believe it or not, that really hurt his campaign, and eventually his momentum just sort of fizzled out. The frontrunner throughout the Democratic primaries was John Kerry, a U.S. Senator from Massachusetts. Kerry was a safe choice for the Democrats- he had moderate views like Bill Clinton. However, he was probably more boring than Clinton. While Kerry had voted for the Iraq War, he had criticized Bush's handling of it and preferred Bush used more diplomacy and less bombs. By Super Tuesday, no one else had a chance. John Kerry was the nominee. Kerry chose John Edwards as his running mate.

So it was George and Dick versus the Johns. Most of the talk leading up to the election was about foreign policy. On the campaign trail, Bush criticized Kerry as a flip flopper on issues, and he tried to convince Americans that he was tough on terrorism. Just like Bush's dad did with Dukakis back in 1988, Bush Jr. tried to convince Americans that Kerry was just another Massachusetts liberal.

Kerry's campaign slogan was "stronger at home, respected in the world." This showed Kerry wanted a return to rebuilding the United States as opposed to nation building around the world. Both Bush and Kerry were serving their country during the Vietnam War, but during the campaigns both were attacked about *how* they served. Critics of Bush, who served in the Texas National Guard, claimed he didn't fulfill his military service contract. Critics of Kerry questioned whether or not he really deserved the medals he earned during the war.

Heading into election day, the polls showed it would be another close race. However, four days before Election Day, videos of Osama bin Laden talking trash surfaced on the TV network al Jazeera. After this, Bush's lead in the polls increased by several points.

And here are the results...

George W. Bush won reelection, and as it turns out, the race was not as close as the election of 2000. Bush received 286 electoral votes and 50.7% of the popular vote. John Kerry received 251 electoral votes and 48.3% of the popular vote. Oh, and one faithless elector in Minnesota randomly voted for John Edwards, but accidentally recorded it as "John Ewards."

The electoral map looked pretty close to the 2000 election, actually.

Bush's margin of victory in the popular vote was the smallest ever for a reelected President.

56.7% of the population voted in this election.

Turn the page for the next election, buddy.

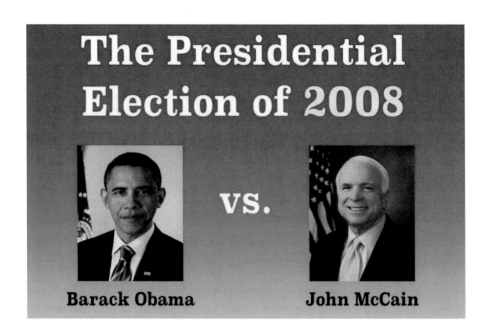

The Presidential Election of 2008

vs.

Barack Obama   **John McCain**

The fifty-sixth Presidential election in American history took place on November 4, 2008. This was the first election in which I voted in the primaries, and there were a lot of exciting candidates to vote for. First, though, let's see how George W. Bush's second term went. Well, probably not that well. The Iraq War kept getting worse, and Bush became a scapegoat for the government's poor response to helping victims affected by Hurricane Katrina. Not only that, but the economy was in shambles after the housing bubble burst in what later became known as The Great Recession.

In 2008, Bush's approval rating had dropped as low as 25%. Therefore, many Republicans began to distance themselves from him. Was Dick Cheney going to run? Haha, that's a good one, Mr. Beat. He was even more unpopular than Bush. This election became the first time since the election of 1952 that neither the current President or current Vice President ended up a candidate, and first time since the election of 1928 that neither even went for it. Then again, Bush couldn't even if he wanted to due to the 22nd Amendment, but anyway...the Republican nomination was completely up for grabs.

I will mention a few folks who ran on the Republican side. First of all, there was Ron Paul, a U.S. Congressman and doctor from Texas, who stood out among the nominees because of his non-interventionist foreign policy and overall libertarian views. He had actually ran for President with the Libertarian Party back in 1988 but had lost badly. There was also Fred Thompson, an actor and former U.S. Senator from Tennessee. There was Rudy Giuliani, the former mayor of New York City. He was mayor, in fact, at the time of the 9/11 attacks, and he liked to bring that up. There was Mike Huckabee, the charismatic former governor of Arkansas who was great at the bass guitar. There was Mitt Romney, the former governor of Massachusetts and son of George Romney, who was a presidential candidate himself back in 1968. Finally, there was John McCain, who was back for a second-go at it after not getting the nomination back in 2000.

McCain was polling in single digits after he first announced his intention to run, but eventually moved his way up to become the frontrunner. While the early primaries went back and forth, after Super Tuesday there was no stopping McCain. He became the Republican nominee, going with a surprise choice as his running mate. That surprise was Sarah Palin, the Governor of Alaska. She was only the second female to be on the ticket for a major political party in American history, and remains one of the most polarizing political figures in American history.

The Democratic Party also had quite a few candidates. First of all, there was Mike Gravel, a former U.S. Senator from Alaska who appeared to not care at all what people thought about him. There was Bill Richardson, the Governor of New Mexico, who was trying to be the first Hispanic to be President in American history. Then there was Dennis Kucinich, a U.S. Representative from Ohio who was the only one running in 2008 who had the distinction of voting against the Iraq War. There was Joe Biden, the U.S. Senator from Delaware who also ran way back in 1988. There was John Edwards, Kerry's running mate in the 2004 election, Hillary Clinton, the wife of former President Bill Clinton and by this time a U.S. Senator from New York. Finally, there was Barack Obama, a U.S. Senator from Illinois, who was a relative newcomer but made a strong impression giving a speech during the 2004 Democratic Convention. Wow, that's a lot of candidates.

Well, there were really two front runners- Clinton and Obama. The two went back and forth in the primaries, and it got pretty intense. After a 17-month long battle, Obama finally got the superdelegates to his side, and in June Hillary Clinton dropped out of the race. The Democratic Party nominated Obama, who became the first African American to win a major political party's nomination for President in American history. He chose Joe Biden as his running mate.

Much of the debate between the Republicans and Democrats in the presidential race revolved around the Iraq War and the financial crisis. Because Bush was so unpopular, McCain distanced himself from him, although Bush did endorse him. McCain had some blunders during his campaign, like not remembering how many houses he had, but so did his running mate Sarah Palin, who especially came across as ignorant regarding foreign policy.

Similar to the election of 1996, a subtle change versus experience theme existed. Obama, who used the word "change" to sum up his entire campaign, pushed for major reforms like universal health care, and bringing our troops home from overseas. McCain, who, like Bob Dole in 1996 and Ronald Reagan in 1984, was up there in age at 72 years old, but he hoped Americans would vote for someone who had been around and knew the system. Plus, Palin was young, like Obama, so he had that going for him.

Obama generally had passionate supporters, and many of them were younger. Palin also tended to have some passionate supporters as well. The candidates in 2008 all took advantage of social media for the first time, and some of them were able to raise millions of dollars completely online. Ron Paul actually raised more money in one day than any other candidate in American history up to that point. It didn't help him in the long run, though. This was the first election in which YouTube existed, and Obama in particular used this medium well.

The Libertarian Party ran Bob Barr, a former U.S. Representative from Georgia, who sued to prevent McCain and Obama from getting on the ballot in Texas, saying their parties didn't reach the state's deadline. The Texas Supreme Court rejected his lawsuit without giving a reason.

Heading into election day, Obama seemed to have all the momentum and most Americans believed the mainstream media was on his side.

And here are the results...

Barack Obama won, becoming the forty-fourth President in American history. He received 365 electoral votes and 52.9% of the popular vote.

John McCain received 173 electoral votes and 45.7% of the popular vote. It was the highest voter turnout since 1968. Obama overwhelmingly got the vote from voters under 35 years old, while McCain overwhelmingly got the 60 and over vote. According to exit polls, over 95 percent of African Americans voted for Obama. That makes sense, as Obama

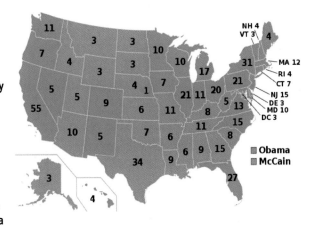

became the first African American President in American history.

Joe Biden became the forty-seventh Vice President in American history.

58.2% of the population voted in this election.

Turn the page for the next election, buddy.

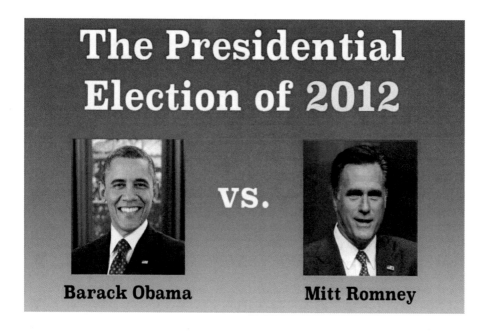

The Presidential Election of 2012

Barack Obama   vs.   **Mitt Romney**

The fifty-seventh Presidential election in American history took place on November 6, 2012, which was my 31st birthday.

Barack Obama became President when the economy really sucked. It was known as the Great Recession, and the Obama administration's solution was to have the federal government micromanage the economy in a way somewhat similar to Franklin Roosevelt's administration. Then again, the George W. Bush administration micromanaged quite a bit, too. Obama continued the bailouts of corporations, but also of ordinary people, and Obama signed laws like the American Recovery and Reinvestment Act to try to get the country out of the recession.

By 2012, the recession was over, but the economy just trudged along. It was nothing to get too excited about. And the rich kept getting richer and the poor kept getting poorer. This led to unrest on both sides of the political spectrum, with The Tea Party movement on the right, and Occupy Wall Street on the left.

Still, Obama kept a campaign promise by bringing the troops home from Iraq. Well, kind of. The United States still has military bases there. Obama did send more troops to fight in Afghanistan, and troops are in fact still there fighting there right now. Obama also sent troops to Libya and expanded the drone strikes in several countries to continue the War on Terrorism, especially in Pakistan. Speaking of Pakistan, on May 1, 2011, U.S. Navy SEALS killed Osama bin Laden, the dude who claimed responsibility for the 9/11 attacks, after they found him hiding seemingly in plain sight there.

Of course, the most famous and probably biggest accomplishment during Obama's term in office was his signing of the Patient Protection and Affordable Care Act, aka Obamacare. The main objectives of the law were to make sure everyone had health insurance and to lower the cost of healthcare.

The Democratic Party still loved Barack Obama, and he was easily renominated, along with Vice President Joe Biden.

The Republican Party, meanwhile, had some division. Yet again, quite a few candidates competed for their nomination. The leading four were former Massachusetts governor Mitt Romney, back again trying for the nomination after not getting it in 2008, U.S. Representative Ron Paul, also back a second time trying for the nomination after not getting it in 2008, Rick Santorum, a former U.S. Senator from Pennsylvania, and Newt Gingrich, the former Speaker of the House, who led the Republican Revolution of 1994. I have to mention that Gingrich used to teach both history and geography at the University of West Georgia.

The Republican candidates had some heated debates and definitely disagreed on several issues. It seemed like it would be tough for the party to unite behind one candidate. However, they somehow did. They nominated Mitt Romney, although many Ron Paul supporters resisted his nomination, and Paul himself did not endorse Romney. Romney was the first Mormon to be nominated by a major party to run for President. Romney picked Paul Ryan, a U.S. Representative from Wisconsin, as his running mate.

The Libertarian Party had gained a lot of momentum, probably because of the popularity of Ron Paul. They nominated Gary Johnson, the former governor of New Mexico, for President, with Jim Gray, a former judge, as his running mate. Johnson originally tried for the Republican nomination but wasn't doing so well so instead joined the Libertarian Party.

However, as you know by now, it's a two-party system lately. The campaigns for Obama and Romney broke records for the amount of money spent and the amount of negative campaigning. This was the first presidential election after the Supreme Court case Citizens United v. FEC, which opened the door for unlimited election spending by corporations. Most of that spending went toward super PACs, or groups trying to drive public policy or get politicians elected without directly working with any candidates or political parties.

At the debates, Romney was critical of Obamacare, even though he was known for Romneycare, which was a similar initiative passed by Romney when he was Governor of Massachusetts.

They also debated foreign policy, but honestly, they didn't disagree too much on the country's role in the world. They did clash on how the government should have responded to the Great Recession. Romney argued the federal government was trying to do too much and making the problem worse, and Obama argued that without the federal government intervening, the recession would have turned into a depression.

Heading into election day, Romney was confident he would win.

And here are the results...

Uh, yeah. Romney didn't win. Barack Obama did, becoming the third President in a row to be reelected. That hadn't happened since 1820 after Monroe, Madison, and Jefferson all got reelected. Obama received 332 electoral votes, and 51.1% of the popular vote. Romney received just 206 electoral votes and 47.2% of the popular vote.

The electoral map looked pretty similar to the 2008 election, although Obama became the first President reelected with fewer electoral votes and less of a popular vote percentage since Franklin Roosevelt in 1944.

Gary Johnson finished with just under 1% of the popular vote.

54.9% of the population voted in this election.

Turn the page for the next election, buddy.

The Presidential Election of 2016

Donald Trump vs. **Hillary Clinton**

The fifty-eighth Presidential election in American history took place on November 8, 2016. The biggest thing Barack Obama could take credit for was a rebounding economy. Just before election day, unemployment was under 5%. Sure, plenty of Americans were underemployed, wealth inequality kept getting worse and worse, and Obamacare was not stopping higher and higher healthcare costs, but at least there was some stability in financial markets and the economy was steadily growing.

Meanwhile, a new Islamic fundamentalist terrorist group called ISIS, or ISIL, armed with American weapons, took over parts of Iraq and Syria. In fact, the world seemed to be a scarier place as more and more terrorists attacked civilians all over the place. Back at home, institutional racism raged on, as it had throughout the entire history of the United States, but now people began fighting back. An entire movement, called Black Lives Matter, rose up to protest against police brutality that seemed to disproportionately affect African Americans.

2016 wasn't as violent as 1968 or 1919, but it sure seemed that way by watching the news. In fact, people were afraid of things that weren't even there.

Perhaps this explains the rise of Donald Trump. Trump had been a celebrity for decades as a very wealthy businessman and reality TV star. He had always flirted with the idea of running for President, but no one had taken him seriously, even when he actually finally announced he was officially running, on June 16, 2015. Few people in the media still didn't take him seriously. He even got criticized for having paid actors to attend to cheer him on at the announcement. But his vague language about making America great again, sounding like a mix between Pat Buchanan, Huey Long, and George Wallace, really resonated with a lot of Americans.

First, though he had to defeat a *lot* of other Republicans wanting the nomination. I will just mention five others, as that's all I have the energy for. There was Jeb Bush, the brother of former President George W. Bush and son of former President George H.W. Bush, and former Governor of Florida. I mean, when both your daddy and your bro were President, you probably should run, right? There was Ben Carson, a retired neurosurgeon originally from Michigan. There was also Marco Rubio, a U.S. Senator from Florida, Ted Cruz, a U.S. Senator from Texas, and John Kasich, the Governor of Ohio.

Just like in 2012, there seemed to be a lot of division within the Republican Party. However, most of the other candidates were soon able to unite against a common enemy- Donald Trump, who, surprisingly, soon became the frontrunner. Because of the Trump effect, candidates often made vicious attacks, and Trump said things never before imagined on the campaign trail. Trump made the debates more exciting to watch with his colorful and sometimes shocking language. The more offensive he seemed to be, the more people seemed to love him. The establishment didn't know what to do.

One by one, the other Republicans went down. Ted Cruz put up the best fight of all. Like Trump, Cruz was also considered an outsider, but Trump was successful at making Cruz seem untrustworthy. He branded him "Lyin' Ted." Yep, despite the naysayers and the Never Trump coalition, Trump won the nomination. He chose Mike Pence, the Governor of Indiana, as his running mate.

The Democratic Party also had division this election. Seemingly before the dawn of time, Hillary Clinton, the now former Secretary of State, was destined to be elected President in 2016. So when she struggled to even get the Democratic nomination, everyone knew this election was different. Bernie Sanders, the independent U.S. Senator from Vermont, put up quite the fight against Clinton. Sanders joined the Democratic Party because he knew from personal experience that running as a third party candidate was so difficult. He was never one who could be easily classified, but one thing was for sure- he leaned further to the left than Clinton. He tried to make "socialism" not such a dirty word anymore.

After Sanders first announced his campaign, the media also didn't take him too seriously. After all, Hillary Clinton was heavily favored. However, his grassroots support quickly grew, especially as he stood in stark contrast to Clinton by not taking donations from corporations, the financial industry, or Super PACs. Sanders and Clinton were neck and neck, going back and forth in early primaries and caucuses. In the end, though, it was Clinton who got the nomination. We now know some shady stuff went down by the establishment Democrats to prevent Bernie from winning. Many of his supporters, especially the younger ones, even refused to support Clinton after she was nominated.

Hillary Clinton was the first female in American history to be nominated for a major political party. *She* nominated Tim Kaine, a U.S. Senator from Virginia and former Governor of Virginia, as her running mate.

So it was Donald Trump versus Hillary Clinton, two of the most unpopular presidential candidates in American history. One poll found that 60 percent of Americans didn't like either candidate. So this was the perfect opportunity for third party candidates, right? Right?

Well, the dude who had the best chance to take on the two major political parties, at least early on, was Gary Johnson, the former governor of New Mexico. He ran in 2012 and got just 1% of the popular vote, but in July he was polling as high as 13 percent nationwide, probably mostly due to the fact that people hated Clinton and Trump so much. Johnson gained more credibility when he got on the ballot in all 50 states, and chose Bill Weld, the respected former Governor of Massachusetts, as his running mate. The two campaigned as a team who hoped to share duties running the country, sort of as a 2-for-1 deal.

Another third party candidate also saw a surge in popularity. Jill Stein, a doctor from Massachusetts, polled as high as 5% in the summer, as many former Sanders supporters now supported her and the Green Party. Stein also ran in 2012 but didn't do so well that time. The Green Party nominated Ajamu Baraka, an activist from Chicago, as her running mate.

However, both Johnson and Stein lacked the money of the Republicans and Democrats, and were attacked quite a bit by the media, bringing up the spoiler myth quite a bit. Johnson certainly didn't help himself when he couldn't think of a world leader he liked, or when he didn't know a city in Syria devastated by the civil war going on there right now. Sure, 95 percent of Americans also didn't know what Aleppo was before this incident, but that didn't matter. The damage was done. Jill Stein was even attacked for beliefs she didn't have.

So most Americans were dreading the results, because they knew it would be either Trump or Clinton. Trump at times seemed a bit racist, misogynistic, and xenophobic, but he appealed to people because he wanted to "Drain the Swamp," meaning get rid of the special interests in Washington. He also ran a masterful campaign. Hillary Clinton had the benefit of not being Trump. Sure, she got associated with being part of the establishment, straight up broke the law by mishandling classified information when she was Secretary of State, and probably had some shady dealings involving the Clinton Foundation. But she spoke in more universal terms and many women were inspired to finally get their chance to vote the first female President into office.

To add to the drama, late in the race a dude named Evan McMullin entered as a last minute attempt for the Never Trump movement. McMullin, a former C.I.A. officer, leaned more conservative but ran as an Independent. His main goal was to win his home state of Utah, and maybe deadlock the Electoral College so that Congress would have to decide the winner. Weeks before the election he was actually beating Clinton and had tied Trump in one poll there.

His running mate was Mindy Finn, a digital media strategist from Texas. According to my research, McMullin and Finn were the second youngest presidential ticket ever, next only to McClellan and Pendleton in 1864.

Clinton was leading in the polls for most the summer and fall, but her lead had tightened right before Election Day.

And here are the results...

This was a squeaker, folks. It wasn't until early the next morning that the majority of the country found out that Donald Trump won, becoming the forty-fifth President in American history. The results frankly shocked the heck out of the majority of the country. The mainstream media especially didn't see it coming, and it was the biggest upset since the election of 1948.

Trump received 304 electoral votes, and Clinton received 227 electoral votes. However, Clinton received nearly 3 million more votes than Trump did overall. She got 48% of the popular vote, while Trump got 46% of the popular vote. Needless to say, a bunch of people began complaining about the Electoral College again. Trump was the fifth person in American history to win the presidency despite losing the popular vote.

In the popular vote, Gary Johnson finished third, with 3.3% of the popular vote, a disappointing finish, but then again it was the best third party finish since Ross Perot in 1996. It was also the Libertarian Party's strongest finish yet. Jill Stein finished fourth, with 1.1%. All other candidates received less than 1 percent. McMullin did win 21.4% of his home state of Utah.

Many called for recounts. Jill Stein led the effort by calling for a recount in Wisconsin, Pennsylvania, and Michigan. Speaking of those three states, ain't nobody saw that coming. Trump won those three states. It was the first time Pennsylvania and Michigan went Republican since 1988, and it was the first time Wisconsin went Republican since 1984.

This election had the highest number of faithless electors, or electors who voted for someone other than their party's nominee, in American history. Seven, faithless electors went against their state and voted differently. Three of them gave votes to Colin Powell, the former Secretary of State under George W. Bush. One gave a vote to Bernie Sanders, although others tried. One gave a vote to John Kasich, one gave a vote to Ron Paul, and one gave a vote to Faith Spotted Eagle, an activist who became the first Native American in American history to receive an electoral vote for President.

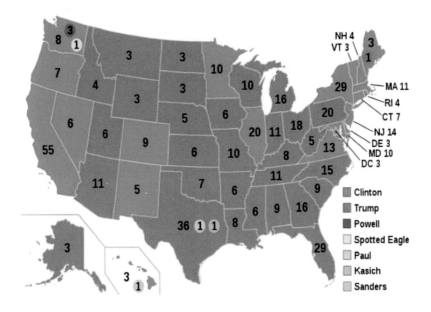

Mike Pence became the forty-eighth Vice President in American history.

This was perhaps the most shocking presidential election result in American history. Even Trump supporters were surprised he pulled it off. Trump became the first President in American history without previous experience in politics, unless you count Zachary Taylor or maybe George Washington. He also became the oldest person ever first elected to the office.

A lot of people ignored his character flaws because they either feared a Clinton presidency more or just wanted an outsider in there to shake things up. Trump voters were hard to categorize, though, which likely explains why the media struggled to predict this one.

55.3% of the population voted in this election.

Turn the page for the next election, buddy.

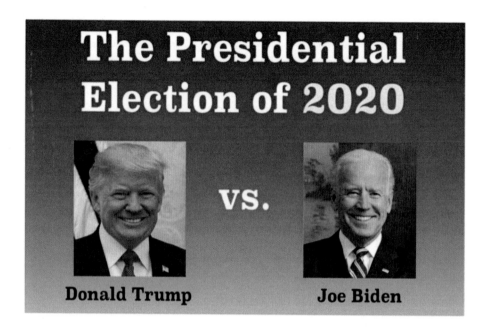

The Presidential Election of 2020

Donald Trump   VS.   Joe Biden

The fifty-ninth Presidential election in American history took place on November 3, 2020. Then again, by that day, a record number of Americans had already voted early- either in person or by mail. You see, for most of the year the world was in the middle of the COVID-19 pandemic. Around 20% of all COVID-19-related deaths in the world happened in the United States, despite the country making up just over 4% of the world's population. By Election Day, it had killed around 235,000 Americans, and many blamed President Donald Trump.

Compared to other world leaders, Trump was slow to respond to the pandemic, and originally downplayed the severity of the virus. Not only that, the economy was doing worse than it had since The Great Depression. Businesses closed and suffered due to lockdowns after local politicians tried to slow the spread of the virus. Unemployment got as high as almost 15%. Despite wages slowly ticking up in the previous three years of the Trump administration, nearly half of all Americans still lived paycheck to paycheck, meaning that when the economy crashed in 2020, they had no savings to get them by.

Trump also became just the third President in American history to be impeached, for abuse of power and obstruction of Congress, after he allegedly tried to get Ukranian officials to dig up dirt on Joe Biden's son to hurt Biden's election campaign. More on that in a bit. Well, the U.S. Senate acquitted Trump, with nearly every Republican voting to keep him in office.

But it wasn't just the impeachment. Throughout all the turmoil of 2020, the Republican Party consistently stood by President Trump. He had a loyal, cult-like following, as seen by his many rallies with enthusiastic supporters. However, Trump also had lots of enemies. Throughout his Presidency, the traditional news media attacked him. Don't worry, he attacked them right back.

Trump lied more than most politicians, so much where it was kind of hard to keep up with all the lies. And he nearly got the country into wars just from seemingly impulsive Tweets. But he also accomplished a lot for conservatives at least attempting to undo much of what Barack Obama accomplished, getting three Supreme Court justice nominees appointed as well as lots of federal judges, lowering taxes, reducing regulations, and beefing up military spending. He even led some bipartisan criminal justice reform. Still, all summer long saw a resurgence of Black Lives Matter protests as police brutality continued to be a big issue, as seen by the horrifying murder of George Floyd.

The Democratic Party...um...did *not* stand by Trump. Throughout his presidency, Trump had been one of the most unpopular Presidents in modern American history, and many Democrats thought they could easily take him. 29 major candidates tried to get their party's presidential nomination, the most for any American political party since 1972.

I will not mention all of them, but I will mention a lot since it was an interesting and diverse group. First of all, there was Tulsi Gabbard, a U.S. Representative from Hawaii. There was Kamala Harris, a U.S. Senator from California- yeah, she dropped out of the race before the primaries began after Gabbard made her look bad due to her history with being tough on drug offenders. There were two candidates who seemingly came out of nowhere- Andrew Yang, an entrepreneur from New York, and Pete Buttigieg, the mayor of South Bend, Indiana. Buttigieg, or Mayor Pete, perhaps since many couldn't pronounce his last name (myself included), was the first openly gay presidential candidate to win a presidential primary or caucus. There were also two billionaires who basically bought their way into the presidential race- Tom Steyer, a New York City hedge fund manager, and Michael Bloomberg, who, after he made *his* billions, was the mayor of New York City. Let's see, who else? There was Amy Klobuchar, a U.S. Senator from Minnesota, Elizabeth Warren, also a U.S. Senator but from Massachusetts. Bernie Sanders was also back. Yep, after basically renewing a progressive movement within the Democratic Party when he ran for President in 2016, the U.S. Senator from Vermont was back with higher support than ever. And finally, there was Joe Biden, the former Vice President who entered the race truly believing he was the only one who could stop Donald Trump, despite the fact that Biden was now 77 years old.

That said, this presidential election had a lot of older folks. Sanders was 78, and so was Bloomberg. Trump was 73. Warren was 70. Hey, it's all good. It was 2020, people were living longer! Just kidding. Sadly, the life expectancy had been going down since the last election.

Well long story short, at first, it looked like Biden *wouldn't* get the nomination, and that Bernie Sanders was, in fact, the front runner. This freaked some people out. Mostly, they got scared of what they thought socialism was and associated Sanders with what they thought socialism was, so all of the candidates who talked trash about "socialism" united against Sanders and threw their support to Biden, who, after winning the South Carolina primary, gained huge momentum and won most delegates after that. Biden became the oldest candidate ever nominated by a major political party, and it was his third time running. He chose Kamala Harris as his running mate, despite the fact that when she ran against him for the nomination she had harshly attacked him in a debate about his past record.

Trump had little opposition getting renominated by the Republicans, although folks like Joe Walsh, a former U.S. Representative from Illinois, and former Massachusetts governor Bill Weld ran against him. You may remember Weld from the 2016 election (he ran for Vice President for the Libertarian Party.) Mike Pence was again Trump's running mate.

After their strongest finish in a presidential election yet in 2016, the Libertarian Party felt confident as it nominated its first female candidate, Jo Jorgensen, a college professor and activist from South Carolina, with Spike Cohen, an activist from Maryland, as her running mate.

Both Trump and Biden were supposed to debate three times, but one of them didn't happen after Trump got COVID and maybe almost died. The first time they debated...that was a bit of a train wreck. It was kind of like two old men yelling at each other.

Mostly due to social media feeds and online echo chambers, the country remained perhaps as divided as it had been since the Civil War. However, throughout his Presidency, Trump's approval rating never really got that high, and even some Republicans, like those who formed the political action committee The Lincoln Project, thought Trump was recklessly leading the country down a path toward fascism.

However, Trump still had tens of millions of loyal followers, who believed every word he said and trusted him with their lives. Despite the COVID-19 pandemic lockdowns, Trump held as many rallies as he could, and many of his supporters showed up not wearing masks, a sign that many of them still downplayed the severity of the virus. On the other side, Biden didn't get out much to campaign, and when he did he had more low-key, kind of boring "rallies" in which supporters stayed in their cars and awkwardly honked their horns at him since he couldn't hear them clapping.

And here are the results...

Joe Biden won, becoming the 46th President in American history.

Biden received 306 electoral votes and 51.3% of the popular vote. Trump received 232 electoral votes and 46.9% of the popular vote.

As divided as the country was, Biden won the largest percentage of the popular vote of any challenger to an incumbent since the election of 1932. Jo Jorgensen finished third with 1.2% of the popular vote.

Kamala Harris became the 49th Vice President in American history, and the first female Vice President in American history. Woahness.

Trump was the first President since George H.W. Bush to not get re-elected.

Biden became the oldest President in American history as soon as he was sworn in. Yep, he was older than Ronald Reagan when Reagan left the Presidency.

Probably at least partially due to the expansion of mail-in voting, this election had the highest voter turnout since the election of 1900. Even though most Americans weren't that excited about Biden, who seemed to be just a return to the status quo, that didn't matter. Most of them seemed to be voting out of fear of four more years of Trump.

Despite it not being that close of an election, Trump refused to say he lost, claiming there was widespread voter fraud. His diehard supporters, of course, *also* absolutely refused to accept the results, believing there was widespread voting fraud. However, Trump's own administration found no evidence of widespread voting fraud, and after dozens of courts (filled with many Trump appointees, I should add) dismissed challenges to the election, many felt the last chance they had to prevent Biden from becoming President was preventing Congress from certifying the electoral vote count. Tragically, on January 6th, the day Congress was supposed to do just that, a mob of hundreds of Trump supporters stormed the U.S. Capitol. Ultimately, five died, including one police officer, and dozens were injured. The rioters occupied, vandalized, and looted the Capitol for hours before the National Guard finally came in to kick them out and make arrests.

Many criticized Trump for inciting the violence and not doing enough to protect the Capitol. He even lost his social media accounts. Yep, not only was his Presidency over, but so was his ability to Tweet to his devoted followers.

Photo credit: Tyler Merbler

Oh, and the House of Representatives impeached him *again*, this time for "incitement of insurrection," making Trump the only American president to be impeached twice.

66.7% of the population voted in this election

Don't worry, I'll see you for the next election, buddy. Follow my YouTube channel, Mr. Beat, for videos over upcoming presidential elections.

Credits, acknowledgements, thank yous

A special thanks to my wife, Shannon (Mrs. Beat), for all of her support over the years as I've made these silly educational videos and put together this book. She has always believed in me, and I couldn't have done any of it without her.

Thanks to my father, Alan Beat (also Mr. Beat), for instilling my love of history and for his help fact-checking and proofreading. Thanks to my mother, Dianna Beat (also Mrs. Beat), for always telling me to pursue my dreams.

Thank you to Fernando Miguel Mercado of the YouTube channel E Pluribus Unum and to American presidential election history expert Ian MacGregor for their additional help fact-checking and proofreading.

All images found in the public domain.
A special shout out to the following for posting helpful graphics into the public domain for use in this book:

AndyHogan14
Cg-realms
Tilden76

Sources for information for this book include:

Dave Leip's Atlas of U.S. Presidential Elections (https://uselectionatlas.org/)

The American Presidency Project (https://www.presidency.ucsb.edu/statistics/elections)

Historical U.S. Presidential Elections 1789-2016 (https://www.270towin.com/)

Our Campaigns (http://www.ourcampaigns.com/)

Made in the USA
Las Vegas, NV
09 August 2023

75763617R00112